BOLOGNA

POCKET TRAVEL GUIDE 2024

Explore History, Culture, Hidden Gems, Cuisine and Local Secrets in the Metropolitan City of Bologna, Emilia-Romagna, Italy – Packed with Detailed Maps & Travel Itineraries

BY

MICHAEL VIANNEY

Copyright © 2024 Michael Vianney. All rights reserved. The entirety of this material, encompassing text, visuals, and other multimedia elements, is the intellectual property of Michael Vianney and is safeguarded by copyright legislation and global agreements. No segment of this content may be replicated, shared, or transmitted in any form or via any medium without explicit written authorization from Michael Vianney. Unauthorized utilization, replication, or dispersal of this content may result in legal repercussions, encompassing civil and criminal penalties. For queries regarding permissions or additional information, kindly contact the author via the provided contact details in the publication or on the author's official page.

TABLE OF CONTENTS

Copyright 1
My Experience in Bologna 5
Benefits of this Guide 8

Chapter 1. Introduction to Bologna 12
1.1 History and Culture 12
1.2 Geography, Climate and Best Time to Visit 14
1.3 Overview of Bologna Neighborhood 16
1.3 Local Customs and Etiquette 18

Chapter 2. Accommodation Options 20
2.1 Hotels and Guesthouses 21
2.2 Bed & Breakfasts and Inns 23
2.3 Apartment Rentals and Vacation Homes 26
2.4 Hostels and Budget Accommodations 28
2.5 Unique Stays: Farmhouses and Vineyard Retreats 30

Chapter 3. Transportation in Bologna 34
3.1 Getting to Bologna 34
3.1 Public Transport: Buses and Trains 36
3.2 Biking in Bologna 38
3.3 Taxis and Ride-Sharing Services 41
3.4 Car Rentals and Driving Tips 44

Chapter 4. Top 10 Hidden Gem Attractions 47
4.1 Santo Stefano Complex 48
4.2 Basilica di San Domenico 51
4.3 Giardini Margherita 53
4.4 Archiginnasio of Bologna 55
4.5 Museum of Modern Art of Bologna (MAMbo) 57

4.6 Bologna Food Markets: Mercato di Mezzo, Mercato delle Erbe..................59
4.7 Oratory of Santa Cecilia..................60
4.8 Portico di San Luca..................62
4.9 Villa Ghigi Park..................64
4.10 Bologna Canals and Bridges..................66
4.11 Sports, Outdoor Activities and Adventures..................68
4.12 Recommended Tour Operators and Guided Tours..................70

Chapter 5 Practical Information and Travel Resources..................73
5.1 Maps and Navigation..................74
5.2 Five Days Itinerary..................75
5.3 Essential Packing List..................79
5.4 Visa Requirements and Entry Procedures..................82
5.5 Safety Tips and Emergency Contacts..................84
5.6 Currency Exchange and Banking Services..................86
5.7 Language, Communication and Useful Phrases..................89
5.8 Shopping and Souvenirs..................91
5.9 Health and Wellness Centers..................94
5.10 Useful Websites, Mobile Apps and Online Resources..................96
5.11 Internet Access and Connectivity..................98
5.12 Visitor Centers and Tourist Assistance..................100

Chapter 6. Culinary Delights..................103
6.1 Traditional Bolognese Cuisine..................103
6.2 Local Delicacies: Mortadella, Crescentine..................105
6.3 Enogastronomic Tours and Wine Tastings..................107
6.4 Gelato and Pasticcerie: Sweet Treats in Bologna..................109
6.5 Michelin-Starred Restaurants and Gastronomic Experiences..................112

Chapter 7. Day Trips and Excursions..................116
7.1 Modena and the Ferrari Museum..................117
7.2 Ravenna and its Mosaics..................118

7.3 Parma and its Culinary Heritage 119
7.4 Ferrara and the Este Castle 121
7.5 Florence: The Cradle of the Renaissance 122

Chapter 8. Entertainment and Nightlife 125
8.1 Piazza Maggiore: Cafés and Aperitivo Spots 125
8.2 Live Music Venues and Jazz Clubs 127
8.3 Teatro Comunale di Bologna: Opera and Theater Performances 129
8.4 Bars and Wine Bars 131
8.5 Festivals and Events 133
Conclusion and Recommendations 136

MY EXPERIENCE IN BOLOGNA

My journey to Bologna was not just another trip; it was an immersion into a world where every corner tells a story, every meal is a celebration, and every experience leaves an indelible mark on your soul. As I arrived in Bologna, the first thing that struck me was the city's unique character. Unlike the more touristy spots in Italy, Bologna feels lived-in and authentic. The city's medieval towers, porticoes, and red-bricked buildings provide a stunning backdrop to daily life, and as I walked through the narrow, cobbled streets, I felt as though I had stepped back in time.

The first morning in Bologna, I wandered into the Quadrilatero, the historic market district. The hustle and bustle of vendors selling fresh produce, cheeses, meats, and fish was invigorating. The air was thick with the tantalizing aromas of herbs and spices, mingling with the scent of freshly baked bread. I couldn't resist sampling some mortadella, a local specialty, and was instantly hooked by its delicate flavor. The locals, warm and welcoming, offered tips on where to find the best tortellini, another Bologna delicacy. Speaking of food, Bologna's culinary scene is nothing short of legendary. The city is often referred to as "La Grassa" (The Fat One), and it lives up to this moniker with a vibrant food culture.

I spent an afternoon at a small trattoria, where I savored a plate of tagliatelle al ragù. The pasta, made fresh that morning, was perfectly al dente, and the rich, meaty sauce was a revelation. Each bite was a testament to the care and tradition that goes into Bolognese cooking. Accompanied by a glass of local Sangiovese, it was a meal I will never forget. Beyond the culinary delights, Bologna's cultural heritage is equally impressive. The University of Bologna, founded in 1088, is the oldest university in continuous operation in the world. I took a guided tour of the university's Archiginnasio, once its main building, now a library and anatomical theater. The intricate wooden carvings and frescoes in the Teatro Anatomico, where dissections were once performed, left me in awe of the history and knowledge that had passed through those walls. Another highlight of my trip was climbing the Asinelli Tower. Standing tall at 97 meters, it offers breathtaking views of the city and the surrounding countryside. The climb is not for the faint-hearted, with nearly 500 steps, but the panorama at the top is worth every bit of effort. Gazing out over the terracotta rooftops, I felt a profound connection to Bologna, a city that so effortlessly blends the past with the present.

Bologna is also a city of art and music. The Pinacoteca Nazionale di Bologna houses an impressive collection of Renaissance and Baroque art. Walking through its halls, I was particularly drawn to works by local artists like the Carracci brothers and Guido Reni. The city's vibrant music scene, epitomized by the Teatro Comunale di Bologna, offers everything from classical opera to contemporary performances. I was fortunate enough to attend a concert at this historic venue, and the acoustics and atmosphere were simply magical.

In the evenings, Bologna takes on a different hue. The streets and piazzas come alive with locals and tourists alike, enjoying aperitivos and lively conversation. I spent several nights at Piazza Maggiore, the city's main square, sipping Aperol Spritz and watching the world go by. The square is flanked by some of Bologna's most iconic buildings, including the Basilica di San Petronio and the Palazzo dei Banchi. As the sun set, the square was bathed in a golden glow, creating a picture-perfect moment that will forever be etched in my memory. What makes Bologna truly special, however, is its people. Warm, friendly, and passionate about their city, the Bolognesi embody the spirit of Italian hospitality. From the shopkeepers and restaurateurs to the university students and families, everyone I met was eager to share their love for Bologna. Their pride in their city is infectious, and it's impossible not to be swept up in their enthusiasm.

Leaving Bologna was bittersweet. I had come seeking an authentic Italian experience, and what I found was a city that exceeded my every expectation. Bologna is a place where history and modernity coexist in perfect harmony, where every meal is a feast, and where every street holds a story waiting to be discovered. And as I boarded my train, I knew that I would return to Bologna, a city that had captured my heart and soul in the most unexpected and delightful ways.

BENEFITS OF THIS GUIDE

Bologna offers an experience that captivates every visitor. Whether you're a history enthusiast, a foodie, or an adventure seeker, this guide will provide you with everything you need to make the most of your visit. Welcome to the ***"Bologna Pocket Travel Guide 2024"*** – your ultimate resource for exploring this enchanting city.

Maps and Navigation

Navigating Bologna is a breeze with its well-preserved medieval layout and modern amenities. The city center, characterized by its narrow, cobbled streets and porticos, is best explored on foot. Detailed maps, both physical and digital, are readily available. Key landmarks such as Piazza Maggiore, the Two Towers (Le Due Torri), and the University of Bologna serve as excellent reference points. For those who prefer digital navigation, apps like Google Maps and Citymapper offer real-time guidance, making it easy to find your way around.

Accommodation Options

Bologna caters to a wide range of accommodation preferences, from luxurious hotels to cozy bed and breakfasts, and budget-friendly hostels. High-end travelers will appreciate the elegance of Grand Hotel Majestic Già Baglioni, offering opulent rooms and top-notch service. Mid-range options like Hotel Metropolitan provide comfort and convenience, often featuring stylish décor and modern amenities. For budget-conscious visitors, hostels such as We_Bologna offer clean, affordable lodgings with communal spaces that foster social interaction.

Transportation

Bologna boasts an efficient public transportation system, including buses and trains that connect the city to the broader Emilia-Romagna region and beyond.

The central train station, Bologna Centrale, is a major hub, making it easy to explore other Italian cities. Buses and taxis are readily available, but many visitors find that walking or renting a bicycle is the best way to experience the city's charm. For those arriving by air, Bologna Guglielmo Marconi Airport offers convenient access to the city center via a short bus ride or taxi.

Top Attractions

Bologna's attractions are diverse and plentiful. Start with Piazza Maggiore, the city's main square, surrounded by historic buildings like the Basilica di San Petronio and the Palazzo dei Notai. The Two Towers, Asinelli and Garisenda, offer breathtaking views of the city for those willing to climb their steep steps. Don't miss the University of Bologna, the oldest university in the world, which adds an academic vibrancy to the city. Art lovers should visit the Pinacoteca Nazionale di Bologna, home to an impressive collection of Renaissance art.

Practical Information and Travel Resources

Before embarking on your Bologna adventure, equip yourself with practical information. The local currency is the Euro, and ATMs are widely available. Italian is the official language, but English is commonly spoken in tourist areas. Tourist information centers, located at key points like Piazza Maggiore, provide maps, brochures, and helpful advice. Consider purchasing a Bologna Welcome Card, which offers free entry to museums, guided tours, and public transport discounts.

Culinary Delights

Bologna is a paradise for food lovers, often referred to as the gastronomic capital of Italy. The city's culinary scene is anchored by its rich tradition of pasta making, with tagliatelle al ragù (Bolognese sauce) being a must-try. Visit the Quadrilatero market area to sample local cheeses, cured meats, and fresh produce. Trattorias and osterias abound, offering authentic dishes in a convivial atmosphere. Don't miss out on trying mortadella, tortellini, and the region's renowned balsamic vinegar.

Culture and Heritage

Bologna's cultural heritage is deeply rooted in its history and academic prominence. The city hosts numerous festivals and events, such as the Bologna Children's Book Fair and the Cinema Ritrovato, celebrating literary and cinematic achievements. Explore the rich architectural tapestry, from medieval towers to Renaissance palaces. The city's museums and galleries offer insights into its artistic and historical evolution, with special attention to local artists and intellectuals who have shaped its legacy.

Outdoor Activities and Adventures

For those seeking outdoor activities, Bologna offers plenty of options. The surrounding hills provide excellent hiking trails with panoramic views of the city. Parks like Giardini Margherita offer a green oasis for picnics, jogging, and leisurely strolls. Adventure enthusiasts can explore the Apennine Mountains nearby, which offer opportunities for skiing, mountain biking, and rock climbing.

Shopping

Bologna's shopping scene is diverse, ranging from high-end boutiques to charming local markets. Via dell'Indipendenza is the main shopping street, featuring a mix of international brands and Italian fashion houses. For a more traditional shopping experience, visit the Quadrilatero district, where you can find artisanal products, gourmet foods, and unique souvenirs. The weekly markets, such as Mercato delle Erbe, offer a glimpse into local life and provide a treasure trove of fresh produce and handmade goods.

Day Trips and Excursions

Bologna's central location makes it an ideal base for exploring other parts of Italy. Take a day trip to the picturesque towns of Modena and Parma, renowned for their culinary specialties. The enchanting city of Florence is just an hour away by train, offering world-famous art and architecture. For nature lovers, the nearby Po River Delta and the Adriatic coast provide beautiful landscapes and recreational opportunities.

Entertainment and Nightlife

Bologna's nightlife is vibrant and varied, catering to all tastes. The city's student population ensures a lively atmosphere, with numerous bars, pubs, and clubs offering entertainment until the early hours. Theaters such as Teatro Comunale di Bologna host opera, ballet, and concerts for those seeking cultural enrichment. Jazz clubs, live music venues, and open-air concerts add to the dynamic nightlife scene, ensuring there is always something happening after dark.

CHAPTER 1
INTRODUCTION TO BOLOGNA

1.1 History and Culture

Bologna, the proud capital of Italy's Emilia-Romagna region, is a city where history and culture merge in a harmonious blend. Its origin story is deeply intertwined with the very fabric of Western civilization. The city's roots stretch back to the Etruscans, who first settled here around the 6th century BCE, calling it Felsina. This was a time when the lush plains of the Po Valley began to witness the rise of a significant urban center. Later, under Roman dominion, it was renamed Bononia in 189 BCE and blossomed into a pivotal trade and cultural hub. Walking through Bologna's streets today, you can feel the echoes of centuries past. The ancient Roman grid layout still influences the city's design, a testament to its long-standing historical continuity. The two iconic towers, Asinelli and Garisenda, rise above the cityscape, emblems of Bologna's medieval ambition and prosperity. These towers are more than just architectural feats; they are symbols of the city's resilience and its citizens' determination to reach for the skies.

The cultural background of Bologna is equally compelling. The University of Bologna, founded in 1088, is widely recognized as the oldest university in the Western world. This institution has been a beacon of knowledge for centuries, drawing scholars from all over Europe and fostering a culture of intellectual pursuit. The university's influence permeates the city, infusing it with a vibrant, youthful energy that contrasts beautifully with its ancient roots. Bologna's cultural life extends beyond its academic achievements. The city is renowned for its culinary heritage, often considered the gastronomic capital of Italy. The rich flavors of traditional Bolognese cuisine, from the hearty ragù to the delicate tortellini, are a reflection of the city's agricultural bounty and the ingenuity of its people. Each meal in Bologna is an invitation to partake in a centuries-old tradition of culinary excellence, where every bite tells a story of the land and its history.

The city's artistic heritage is equally illustrious. Bologna boasts an array of art galleries, museums, and historic sites that capture the essence of its rich cultural tapestry. The Basilica di San Petronio, located in Piazza Maggiore, is one of the largest churches in the world and stands as a monument to the city's architectural prowess and religious devotion. Meanwhile, the Archiginnasio, once the main building of the University of Bologna, now houses the Biblioteca Comunale, a treasure trove of ancient manuscripts and books that narrate the intellectual journey of humanity. In every corner of Bologna, there is a story waiting to be discovered. The city's porticoes, stretching for miles, offer not just shelter from the elements but a glimpse into the communal spirit of its people. These covered walkways have witnessed countless moments of everyday life, from market exchanges to scholarly debates, creating a unique sense of continuity and connection across generations.

1.2 Geography, Climate and Best Time to Visit

Bologna, the vibrant capital of Italy's Emilia-Romagna region, is a city of rich history and stunning landscapes. In the heart of the Po Valley, Bologna's geography is characterized by its strategic location between the rolling hills of the Apennines and the fertile plains that stretch north towards the River Po. This unique positioning not only makes Bologna a natural crossroad of culture and commerce but also endows it with a diverse and appealing climate that changes beautifully with the seasons.

Geography of Bologna

Bologna is strategically situated in northern Italy, making it a vital connection point between the northern and southern parts of the country. The city is roughly halfway between Florence and Venice, and its central location means that it is well-connected by rail and road, making it accessible from various parts of Italy and Europe. The terrain of Bologna is predominantly flat in the city center, but as you move south, the landscape begins to rise gently into the foothills of the Apennine Mountains. This topographical diversity not only provides stunning vistas but also influences the local climate and agriculture.

Climate of Bologna

Bologna experiences a humid subtropical climate, marked by hot summers and cool, damp winters. The city's climate can be divided into four distinct seasons, each offering its own unique charm and opportunities for visitors.

Spring (March to May)

Spring in Bologna is a delightful time to visit. The season is characterized by mild temperatures and blooming flowers, making the city's gardens and parks particularly inviting. Average temperatures range from 10°C (50°F) in March to 20°C (68°F) in May. Rainfall is moderate, but the occasional spring shower only adds to the fresh and vibrant atmosphere. The pleasant weather makes it ideal for exploring Bologna's historical sites, enjoying outdoor cafes, and strolling through the scenic countryside.

Summer (June to August)

Summers in Bologna are typically hot and humid, with temperatures often reaching 30°C (86°F) and above in July and August. While the heat can be intense, the city's many shaded porticoes provide some relief. Summer is also a vibrant time in Bologna, with numerous festivals, outdoor concerts, and events. Evening temperatures cool down, creating perfect conditions for enjoying Bologna's lively nightlife and dining alfresco. For those who find the heat challenging, early mornings and late evenings are the best times to explore the city.

Autumn (September to November)

Autumn is arguably the best time to visit Bologna. The weather is comfortably warm in September and October, with temperatures ranging from 20°C (68°F) to 25°C (77°F), before gradually cooling down in November. The fall colors add a magical touch to the city and its surrounding countryside. This season is also harvest time, making it the perfect opportunity to savor Bologna's renowned culinary offerings, including fresh truffles, chestnuts, and local wines. The combination of mild weather and cultural events makes autumn a favorite season for many visitors.

Winter (December to February)

Winters in Bologna are cool and damp, with average temperatures ranging from 1°C (34°F) to 7°C (45°F). While snow is rare, the city does experience regular rainfall. Despite the cooler weather, winter has its own appeal. The city's historic architecture and festive decorations during the Christmas season create a cozy and enchanting atmosphere. It's also a great time to indulge in hearty

Bolognese cuisine, warming up with rich ragù, fresh pasta, and robust local wines.

Best Times to Visit Bologna

The best time to visit Bologna largely depends on your personal preferences and interests. However, many travelers find that spring (March to May) and autumn (September to November) offer the most favorable conditions. These seasons provide mild weather, fewer tourists, and a range of cultural and culinary experiences. In spring, the city's gardens and parks are in full bloom, and outdoor festivals begin to take place. This is an excellent time for sightseeing and enjoying the natural beauty of the region. Autumn, on the other hand, offers the perfect blend of warm weather and culinary delights. The harvest season brings with it a bounty of fresh produce and local specialties, and the city's cultural calendar is filled with events and festivals celebrating food, music, and art. For those who enjoy warmer weather and vibrant city life, summer offers a range of outdoor activities and events, although it's essential to be prepared for the heat. Winter, while quieter, allows for a more intimate experience of Bologna's historical sites and culinary treasures, without the crowds.

1.3 Overview of Bologna Neighborhood

Bologna is a city that invites you to wander its vibrant neighborhoods, each with its own distinct personality and charm. Exploring these areas is like stepping into different worlds, each offering unique experiences that make Bologna such a captivating destination. Whether you are drawn to historic landmarks, culinary delights, or lively social scenes, the neighborhoods of Bologna promise a rich and rewarding journey.

Centro Storico: Centro Storico, or the historic center, is the beating heart of Bologna. This neighborhood encapsulates the essence of the city, where every corner tells a story of its rich past. Here, you can stroll through the grand Piazza

Maggiore, the city's main square, flanked by the impressive Basilica di San Petronio and the medieval Palazzo del Podestà. The iconic Two Towers, Asinelli and Garisenda, dominate the skyline and offer panoramic views for those willing to climb their steep staircases.

Santo Stefano: Santo Stefano is a neighborhood that exudes a bohemian charm, perfect for those seeking a more relaxed and artistic atmosphere. The area is named after the Basilica di Santo Stefano, a complex of seven churches that form one of Bologna's most fascinating religious sites. The piazza in front of the basilica is a popular gathering spot, where locals and visitors alike sit and enjoy the tranquil surroundings.

Navile: Navile is where the academic pulse of Bologna is most strongly felt. This neighborhood is home to the University of Bologna, the oldest university in the world, and its presence permeates the entire area. The streets are filled with students, and the atmosphere is one of intellectual curiosity and youthful energy. The university buildings themselves are architectural marvels, steeped in history and academic prestige.

Quadrilatero: For those who are drawn to the sensory delights of food and shopping, Quadrilatero is the neighborhood that will captivate your senses. Located just off Piazza Maggiore, this historic market district is a labyrinth of narrow streets filled with food stalls, delicatessens, and artisanal shops. The aroma of freshly baked bread, cured meats, and aged cheeses fills the air, inviting you to indulge in Bologna's renowned culinary heritage.

Bolognina: Bolognina, located just north of the city center, represents the modern and multicultural side of Bologna. This neighborhood has undergone significant transformation and is now a melting pot of cultures, reflected in its diverse population and eclectic mix of shops and restaurants. The streets of

Bolognina are alive with the sounds and flavors of different cultures, making it a vibrant and dynamic area to explore.

1.3 Local Customs and Etiquette
Each of these customs offers a window into the soul of Bologna, revealing a city that cherishes its traditions and celebrates human connection. From the lively aperitivo gatherings to the communal experience of the Mercato di Mezzo, from the reverence for music at Teatro Comunale to the spiritual celebrations of San Petronio, and the intimate Sunday family lunches, Bologna invites visitors to become part of its rich, living tapestry.

The Warmth of the Aperitivo: In Bologna, the aperitivo is more than just a pre-dinner drink; it's a cherished daily ritual that encapsulates the city's vibrant social life. As the evening approaches, the city's bars and piazzas fill with people ready to unwind. In Piazza Santo Stefano, friends and families gather, enjoying local wines and an assortment of small bites. This time-honored tradition is not just about food and drink, but about relishing the company of loved ones and celebrating the end of another day. It's a quintessentially Bolognese way to savor life's simple pleasures, offering visitors a genuine taste of the city's convivial spirit.

The Vibrant Mercato di Mezzo: A visit to the Mercato di Mezzo is a journey into the heart of Bologna's culinary soul. This historic market, located in the Quadrilatero district, is a lively hub where vendors and locals engage in animated exchanges. Shopping here is an interactive experience, where buying groceries turns into a social event. The market's atmosphere, filled with the scents of fresh produce and the sounds of friendly haggling, reflects the Bolognese love for food and community. It's a place where culinary traditions are not just preserved but celebrated, offering a vivid glimpse into the city's daily life.

The Reverence for Music at Teatro Comunale: Bologna's deep appreciation for the arts is palpable at the Teatro Comunale di Bologna, situated in Piazza Verdi. This historic opera house is more than a venue; it's a cultural landmark where the city's love for music and performance shines brightly. Attending an opera or symphony here is an immersive experience, with the audience's enthusiastic reactions adding to the performance's magic. The communal experience of enjoying music at Teatro Comunale reflects Bologna's rich artistic heritage and the city's enduring connection to its cultural roots.

The Spiritual Festivities of San Petronio: The Feast of San Petronio, held every October 4th, is a profound expression of Bologna's religious and historical identity. This celebration in honor of the city's patron saint transforms the Basilica di San Petronio in Piazza Maggiore into the heart of the festivities. The event includes processions, masses, and communal feasts, blending religious observance with community celebration. The feast day offers a unique opportunity to witness Bologna's spiritual devotion and its residents' deep sense of tradition, providing visitors with a deeper understanding of the city's cultural fabric.

The Tradition of Sunday Family Lunches: One of Bologna's most endearing customs is the Sunday family lunch, a weekly tradition that underscores the importance of family and home-cooked meals. These lunches are intimate gatherings where generations come together to share stories and enjoy traditional dishes. In the warmth of Bolognese homes, the air is filled with the comforting aromas of ragù and the sounds of lively conversation. This tradition highlights the Bolognese belief in the power of food to bring people together, offering a heartfelt glimpse into the city's familial bonds and culinary heritage.

CHAPTER 2
ACCOMMODATION OPTIONS

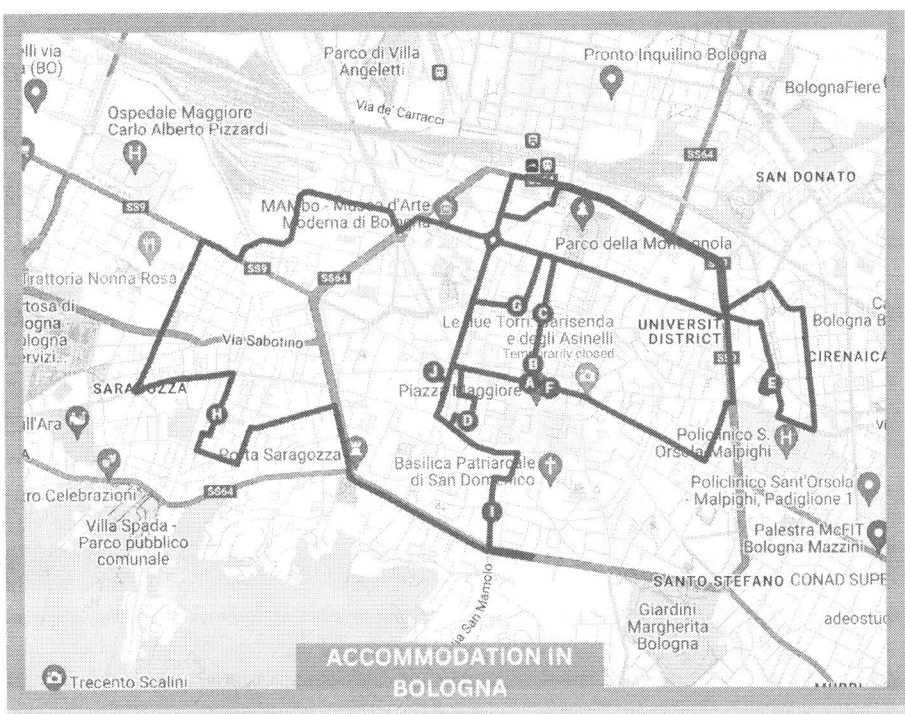

Directions from Bologna, Metropolitan City of Bologna, Italy to Via del Pratello, 8, Bologna, Metropolitan City of Bologna, Italy

A	E	H
Bologna, Metropolitan City of Bologna, Italy	Aemilia Hotel, Via Zaccherini Alvisi, Bologna, Metropolitan City of Bologna, Italy	Il Giardino nel Parco R&B, Via Edoardo Brizio, Bologna, Metropolitan City of Bologna, Italy
B		
Grand Hotel Majestic già Baglioni, Via dell'Indipendenza, Bologna, Metropolitan City of Bologna, Italy		
C	**F**	**I**
Hotel Metropolitan, Via dell'Orso, Bologna, Metropolitan City of Bologna, Italy	Luxury B&B Casa Faccioli, Via Caduti di Cefalonia, Bologna, Metropolitan City of Bologna, Italy	Antica Residenza D'Azeglio, Via d'Azeglio, Bologna, Metropolitan City of Bologna, Italy
D	**G**	**J**
Bologna nel Cuore B&B e Suite di Charme, Via Cesare Battisti, Bologna, Metropolitan City of Bologna, Italy	Bed & Breakfast La piazzetta della pioggia, Via Riva di Reno, Bologna, Metropolitan City of Bologna, Italy	Via del Pratello, 8, Bologna, Metropolitan City of Bologna, Italy

2.1 Hotels and Guesthouses

Bologna offers a variety of accommodations ranging from luxurious hotels to cozy guesthouses. Whether you're a business traveler, a history enthusiast, or a culinary explorer, Bologna has something to offer for everyone. Here, we delve into exceptional accommodations in Bologna, each offering a unique experience, exceptional amenities, and the warmth of Italian hospitality.

Grand Hotel Majestic "Già Baglioni"

Located on Via Indipendenza, the Grand Hotel Majestic "Già Baglioni" stands as a beacon of luxury and elegance in Bologna. This five-star hotel, housed in an 18th-century palazzo, combines classic architecture with modern amenities, creating an atmosphere of timeless sophistication. Guests can expect to pay approximately €300 to €600 per night, depending on the room type and season. The hotel offers a range of luxurious amenities including a state-of-the-art fitness center, a spa, and an on-site gourmet restaurant, "I Carracci," known for its exquisite Italian cuisine. Unique features of the hotel include original frescoes, antique furniture, and a stunning marble staircase. The hotel also provides concierge services, ensuring that guests have access to tailored experiences such as private city tours and exclusive dining reservations. For more information and bookings, visitors can access the official website: (https://www.grandhotelmajestic.it).

Hotel Metropolitan

In the heart of Bologna's historic center, Hotel Metropolitan offers a blend of contemporary style and traditional Italian hospitality. Situated on Via dell'Orso, this boutique hotel is a short walk from Piazza Maggiore and the Two Towers. The price range for rooms typically varies between €120 and €250 per night.

Hotel Metropolitan is known for its modern décor, featuring sleek lines and vibrant colors. The rooftop terrace provides a serene escape with panoramic views of the city, and the hotel's bar offers a selection of fine wines and cocktails. Complimentary services include a hearty Italian breakfast and high-speed Wi-Fi. The hotel also offers guided tours and bike rentals for guests wishing to explore the city more intimately. Guests can find more details and make reservations on the official website: (https://www.hotelmetropolitan.com).

Art Hotel Novecento

Art Hotel Novecento, located on Piazza Galileo, is a boutique hotel that exudes charm and artistic flair. This four-star accommodation is designed with an eclectic mix of modern and Art Nouveau styles, offering guests a visually stimulating environment. The room rates generally range from €150 to €300 per night. The hotel's unique features include individually decorated rooms with original artwork and modern amenities such as flat-screen TVs and minibars. The hotel offers a complimentary breakfast buffet with a variety of local delicacies and fresh pastries. Special services include a 24-hour front desk, airport transfers, and personalized city tours. Additionally, Art Hotel Novecento is pet-friendly, welcoming guests traveling with their furry companions. For further information and reservations, visit the official website: (https://www.arthotelnovecento.it).

B&B Bologna nel Cuore

For travelers seeking a more intimate and homely experience, B&B Bologna nel Cuore offers a delightful stay in a charming guesthouse setting. Located on Via Cesare Battisti, this bed and breakfast is just a stone's throw from the major attractions of Bologna. Room prices typically range from €90 to €150 per night, making it an affordable yet cozy option. B&B Bologna nel Cuore prides itself on its personalized service and welcoming atmosphere. The rooms are elegantly furnished with a mix of antique and modern pieces, and guests are treated to a homemade breakfast featuring local and organic ingredients. The hosts provide valuable insights into local attractions and dining options, ensuring guests have a memorable stay. The guesthouse also offers free Wi-Fi, and rooms are equipped with air conditioning and private bathrooms. More information and booking options can be found on their official website: (https://www.bolognanelcuore.com).

Aemilia Hotel Bologna

Aemilia Hotel Bologna, located on Via Giovanna Zaccherini Alvisi, offers a contemporary and comfortable stay with easy access to the city center and major landmarks. The hotel's room rates range from €100 to €200 per night, catering to both business and leisure travelers. The hotel features spacious rooms with modern amenities such as flat-screen TVs, minibars, and complimentary Wi-Fi. Guests can enjoy the on-site restaurant, which serves a variety of Italian and international dishes, as well as a daily breakfast buffet. Unique to Aemilia Hotel is its large terrace, offering spectacular views of the city, and a wellness area equipped with a gym and a hot tub. Special services include meeting and conference facilities, making it an ideal choice for business travelers. The hotel also offers bike rentals for guests who wish to explore Bologna on two wheels. For more details and reservations, the official website is: (https://www.aemiliahotel.it).

2.2 Bed & Breakfasts and Inns

Bologna offers travelers an array of accommodations that reflect its charm and character, particularly in its Bed & Breakfasts and Inns. These establishments provide a unique blend of comfort, personalized service, and local flavor, making them an ideal choice for visitors seeking an authentic Bolognese experience. In this detailed exploration, we will delve into five distinctive Bed & Breakfasts and Inns in Bologna, highlighting their locations, amenities, special features, and other essential information to help you plan your stay.

B&B Casa Faccioli

B&B Casa Faccioli offers guests a unique blend of history and modern comfort. This charming B&B is located just a stone's throw away from Piazza Maggiore, making it an excellent base for exploring the city's main attractions. Casa Faccioli boasts elegantly furnished rooms that feature antique furniture, original frescoes, and modern amenities like air conditioning, free Wi-Fi, and flat-screen TVs. The starting price for lodging at Casa Faccioli is approximately €120 per night, including a hearty continental breakfast. One of the standout features of this B&B is its rooftop terrace, which provides a breathtaking view of Bologna's red-tiled rooftops and historic landmarks. Guests can also enjoy a delightful breakfast in the cozy dining area or, weather permitting, on the terrace. Casa Faccioli is committed to providing personalized services, including arranging guided city tours, cooking classes, and wine tastings. For more information and reservations, you can visit their official website at (https://www.casafaccioli.com).

B&B La Piazzetta della Pioggia

B&B La Piazzetta della Pioggia is a cozy and welcoming establishment located near Bologna's vibrant Via Indipendenza and a short walk from the train station. This B&B offers a peaceful retreat with its elegantly decorated rooms, each equipped with modern comforts such as free Wi-Fi, air conditioning, and private bathrooms. The accommodation prices start at around €90 per night, including a continental breakfast featuring local products. What sets La Piazzetta della Pioggia apart is its focus on creating a homely atmosphere for guests. The common lounge area is perfect for relaxing after a day of sightseeing, and the friendly hosts are always ready to provide recommendations for dining and entertainment. Guests can take advantage of additional services such as airport transfers, bike rentals, and laundry service. For further details and to make a reservation, visit (https://www.lapiazzettadellapioggia.com).

Il Giardino Nel Parco

Il Giardino Nel Parco, which translates to "The Garden in the Park," lives up to its name with a serene garden setting just outside Bologna's historical center. This tranquil B&B is ideal for those who wish to enjoy the city's sights while staying in a more relaxed, green environment. The property offers stylishly furnished rooms with garden views, equipped with amenities like free Wi-Fi, air conditioning, and flat-screen TVs. Rooms at Il Giardino Nel Parco start at approximately €85 per night, with breakfast included. The B&B's garden is a highlight, providing a perfect spot for morning coffee or an evening aperitif. Guests are treated to a generous breakfast with a selection of organic and locally sourced products, served either in the garden or in the charming dining room. Il Giardino Nel Parco offers personalized services such as yoga sessions, massage therapy, and cooking classes. To learn more or to book a stay, visit their website at (https://www.ilgiardinonelparco.com).

Antica Residenza D'Azeglio

Situated in a beautiful 19th-century building in the historic center, Antica Residenza D'Azeglio combines elegance with modern comfort. This inn is just a few minutes' walk from Bologna's main attractions, including Piazza Maggiore and the Two Towers. The rooms are spacious and tastefully decorated, featuring antique furnishings, free Wi-Fi, air conditioning, and private bathrooms. The nightly rates at Antica Residenza D'Azeglio start at around €110, inclusive of a rich breakfast served in the sophisticated dining room. A notable feature of this inn is its library, which offers a quiet space for guests to relax with a book. Additionally, the staff is known for their warm hospitality and are always eager to assist with booking tours, restaurant reservations, and providing local insights. For more information and reservations, visit (https://www.anticaresidenzadazeglio.it).

B&B Pratello 8

Located in the lively and bohemian Pratello neighborhood, B&B Pratello 8 offers a unique and vibrant stay. This area is known for its eclectic mix of cafes, bars, and cultural spots, making it a favorite among younger travelers and those looking to experience Bologna's nightlife. The B&B itself features contemporary decor with comfortable rooms equipped with free Wi-Fi, air conditioning, and flat-screen TVs. Accommodation at Pratello 8 is competitively priced, with rates starting at approximately €70 per night, including a continental breakfast. One of the unique features of this B&B is its emphasis on sustainability; they use eco-friendly products and encourage guests to adopt green practices during their stay. Pratello 8 provides additional services such as bike rentals, guided city tours, and a communal kitchen where guests can prepare their own meals. The hosts are known for their friendly and helpful demeanor, ensuring that every guest feels at home. For more details and to book a stay, visit (https://www.pratello8.com).

2.3 Apartment Rentals and Vacation Homes

Bologna offers a variety of accommodations that cater to different tastes and budgets. For those looking to immerse themselves fully in the Bolognese experience, staying in an apartment rental or vacation home can provide a more authentic and intimate experience compared to traditional hotels. Here, we explore unique and exceptional properties in Bologna, each offering distinct features and amenities.

Casa Bertagni

Casa Bertagni stands as a testament to luxury and sophistication in the heart of Bologna. Situated just a stone's throw from the University of Bologna and the famous Two Towers, this boutique guest house is perfect for those seeking a blend of elegance and convenience. Prices for lodging at Casa Bertagni start at approximately €200 per night, varying with the season and room choice. Each suite in Casa Bertagni is exquisitely decorated, combining classic and contemporary elements to create a refined ambiance. Amenities include air conditioning, flat-screen TVs, free Wi-Fi, and en-suite bathrooms with luxury toiletries. Unique features of Casa Bertagni include its meticulously curated art collection and bespoke furnishings that evoke a sense of historical charm and modern comfort. For bookings and reservations, visitors can access their official website at (http://www.casabertagni.com).

Palazzo Trevi Charming House

Located in the historic center of Bologna, Palazzo Trevi Charming House is an epitome of comfort and style. Nestled near Piazza Maggiore and the Basilica of San Petronio, this accommodation is perfect for exploring Bologna's historic landmarks. Nightly rates begin at around €150, depending on the time of year and the room type. The rooms and apartments at Palazzo Trevi are designed with a modern flair while retaining traditional touches. Guests can enjoy amenities such as air conditioning, Wi-Fi, satellite TV, and kitchenettes in some units. The unique aspect of Palazzo Trevi is its tranquil courtyard garden, offering a serene escape from the bustling city. For further details and to make reservations, the official website is (http://www.palazzotrevi.it).

Residenza Ariosto

Residenza Ariosto offers a contemporary stay in a central location, just minutes from the iconic Two Towers and Piazza Maggiore. This modern apartment complex provides the comfort of home with the convenience of being in the heart of Bologna. Prices for these stylish apartments start at about €120 per night. Each apartment at Residenza Ariosto is fully furnished with a modern aesthetic, featuring amenities such as free Wi-Fi, flat-screen TVs, fully equipped kitchens, and spacious living areas. The unique selling point of Residenza Ariosto is its home-like atmosphere combined with hotel-like services, such as daily cleaning and concierge support. Guests can enjoy the flexibility of preparing their own meals in the apartment's kitchen or explore the culinary delights of nearby restaurants and markets. For those interested in exploring Bologna's gastronomic scene, the staff can arrange food tours and cooking classes. For bookings and additional information, visit (http://www.residenzaariosto.it).

2.4 Hostels and Budget Accommodations

Bologna boasts luxurious hotels and boutique accommodations, it also offers numerous budget-friendly options for travelers seeking affordability without compromising comfort and quality. Whether you're a backpacker, a student, or simply a budget-conscious traveler, Bologna provides a variety of hostels and budget accommodations that cater to different needs and preferences. In this guide, we explore distinctive budget accommodations in Bologna, highlighting their locations, amenities, prices, and unique features.

We_Bologna Hostel

We_Bologna Hostel, located on Via de' Carracci, is a modern and vibrant hostel that caters to young travelers and backpackers. Situated close to the Bologna Centrale train station, it offers easy access to the city's main attractions. The lodging prices range from €20 for a dorm bed to €70 for a private room, making it an economical choice. The hostel boasts a range of amenities including free Wi-Fi, a fully equipped kitchen, and a spacious common area where guests can socialize and relax. Unique features of We_Bologna include its contemporary design, outdoor garden, and on-site bar. The hostel also provides bicycle rentals, laundry facilities, and a 24-hour reception. Guests can enjoy a complimentary breakfast each morning, and the hostel frequently hosts events and activities, fostering a vibrant community atmosphere. For more information and bookings, visit the official website: (https://www.we-gastameco.com/bologna).

Il Nosadillo

Il Nosadillo, a cozy and intimate hostel, is located on Via Nosadella in the historic center of Bologna. This small guesthouse-style hostel offers a homely atmosphere with prices ranging from €25 for a bed in a shared dormitory to €60 for a private room. The hostel features a communal kitchen where guests can prepare their meals and a comfortable common area for socializing. Unique to Il Nosadillo is its emphasis on creating a family-like environment, with friendly staff and a welcoming ambiance. The hostel offers free Wi-Fi, complimentary breakfast, and lockers for secure storage of belongings. Its central location makes it an ideal base for exploring Bologna's cultural and historical sites. More details and reservations can be found on their official website: (https://www.ilnosadillo.com).

Dopa Hostel

Dopa Hostel, located on Via Irnerio, is a stylish and artistic hostel situated in the university district of Bologna. Known for its colorful décor and vibrant atmosphere, Dopa Hostel offers affordable lodging with prices ranging from €25 for a dorm bed to €80 for a private room. Amenities at Dopa Hostel include free breakfast, Wi-Fi, a communal kitchen, and a lively common area decorated with murals and unique art pieces. The hostel also features a bar where guests can enjoy drinks and snacks. Dopa Hostel provides guided city tours, bike rentals, and organizes regular events such as live music and art exhibitions, making it a hub of creativity and social interaction. For more information and to make reservations, visit the official website: (https://www.dopahostel.com).

Combo Bologna

Combo Bologna, situated on Via De' Carracci, offers a blend of hostel and hotel services in a modern and sleek environment. Located near the train station, it is well-connected to Bologna's main attractions. The prices range from €30 for a dormitory bed to €100 for a private room. The hostel provides numerous amenities including free Wi-Fi, a communal kitchen, a bar, and a restaurant serving local cuisine. Unique features of Combo Bologna include its contemporary design, outdoor terrace, and cultural programming which includes workshops, exhibitions, and performances. Guests can enjoy a variety of services such as laundry facilities, luggage storage, and 24-hour reception. The hostel also offers a breakfast buffet for an additional fee. Further details and bookings can be made on the official website: (https://www.thisiscombo.com).

Ostello San Filippo Neri

Ostello San Filippo Neri, located on Via Santa Caterina, provides a peaceful retreat within the bustling city. This hostel, housed in a historic building, offers a range of affordable accommodation options with prices from €20 for a dorm bed to €70 for a private room. The hostel features amenities such as free Wi-Fi, a communal kitchen, and a tranquil garden where guests can unwind. Unique to Ostello San Filippo Neri is its historical ambiance, complemented by modern comforts. The hostel offers laundry services, luggage storage, and a complimentary breakfast. Its proximity to major attractions makes it an ideal choice for travelers seeking a quiet yet centrally located accommodation. More information and reservations can be found on their official website:(https://www.ostellosanfilipponeri.com).

2.5 Unique Stays: Farmhouses and Vineyard Retreats

Bologna offers more than just conventional hotel stays. For travelers seeking a distinctive experience, Bologna presents an array of unique accommodations such as farmhouses, vineyard retreats, and other special stays that immerse guests in the region's rustic charm and vibrant culture. This exploration delves into exceptional properties, each offering a unique taste of Bologna's countryside and beyond, highlighting their locations, amenities, special features, and other essential information to enhance your travel experience.

Agriturismo Il Cavicchio

Located just a few kilometers from the heart of Bologna, Agriturismo Il Cavicchio offers a serene escape into the countryside while still being conveniently close to the city's attractions. This charming farmhouse is surrounded by lush gardens and vineyards, providing a peaceful retreat for nature lovers. The rooms and apartments at Il Cavicchio are tastefully decorated, blending rustic charm with modern comforts like free Wi-Fi, air conditioning, and private bathrooms. The prices for lodging start at around €100 per night, including a hearty breakfast featuring organic produce from the farm. One of the unique features of Il Cavicchio is its outdoor pool, set amidst the verdant landscape, where guests can unwind and soak in the tranquility. The farmhouse also offers cooking classes, wine tastings, and guided tours of the vineyards, allowing guests to immerse themselves in the local culture and traditions. For more information and to make reservations, visit their official website at (https://www.ilcavicchio.it).

Podere San Giuliano

Podere San Giuliano is a charming farmhouse located in the picturesque countryside just outside Bologna. This agriturismo is renowned for its emphasis on sustainable and organic farming practices, offering guests a unique and eco-friendly stay. The accommodations range from cozy rooms to spacious apartments, all featuring rustic decor and modern amenities like free Wi-Fi, air conditioning, and private bathrooms. Lodging prices start at approximately €90 per night, with a delicious farm-to-table breakfast included. Podere San Giuliano stands out for its culinary offerings; the on-site restaurant serves meals made from fresh, organic ingredients grown on the farm. Guests can also participate in cooking workshops and wine tastings, learning about the farm's sustainable practices and the region's culinary heritage. The property provides additional services such as bike rentals, guided farm tours, and picnic arrangements. For further details and bookings, visit (https://www.poderesangiuliano.it).

Tenuta Bettozza

Tenuta Bettozza is a stunning vineyard retreat that offers breathtaking views and a tranquil environment. This estate is perfect for wine enthusiasts and those looking to experience the beauty of Bologna's wine country. The accommodations at Tenuta Bettozza include elegantly furnished rooms and suites, equipped with modern amenities like free Wi-Fi, air conditioning, and flat-screen TVs. Starting at around €120 per night, the lodging includes a gourmet breakfast served with fresh local products. A highlight of Tenuta Bettozza is its vineyard tours and wine tastings, where guests can explore the vineyards, learn about the winemaking process, and sample the estate's exquisite wines. The retreat also offers cooking classes, allowing guests to master traditional Bolognese recipes. For relaxation, guests can enjoy the outdoor swimming pool and the scenic walking trails around the estate. To learn more or to book a stay, visit (https://www.tenutabettozza.it).

Borgo delle Vigne

Borgo delle Vigne is a captivating vineyard estate located in the heart of the Colli Bolognesi wine region. This unique stay combines luxury with a deep connection to the land, offering guests an immersive experience in one of Bologna's most beautiful landscapes. The estate features stylishly decorated rooms and suites, equipped with free Wi-Fi, air conditioning, and private bathrooms. The prices for lodging at Borgo delle Vigne start at approximately €130 per night, including a sumptuous breakfast. A unique feature of this estate is its focus on wine tourism; guests can participate in extensive vineyard tours, wine tastings, and even grape harvesting during the season. The on-site restaurant offers delectable meals made from locally sourced ingredients, paired with the estate's finest wines. Borgo delle Vigne also provides special services such as private dinners in the vineyard, cooking classes, and wellness treatments. For more information and reservations, visit (https://www.borgodellevigne.com).

Fattoria Belvedere

Located in the rolling hills of Bologna's countryside, Fattoria Belvedere is a picturesque farmhouse offering a tranquil retreat surrounded by nature. This agriturismo provides cozy rooms and apartments with rustic decor, modern amenities like free Wi-Fi, and private bathrooms. The farm's peaceful environment and stunning views make it an ideal choice for relaxation and rejuvenation. Lodging prices at Fattoria Belvedere start at around €80 per night, with a hearty breakfast included. One of the unique features of this farmhouse is its commitment to organic farming; guests can enjoy fresh produce from the farm's gardens and participate in farm activities like cheese making and vegetable picking. The property also features an outdoor pool, perfect for relaxing on warm days. Special services at Fattoria Belvedere include guided nature walks, cooking classes, and horse riding. For further details and to make a reservation, visit (https://www.fattoriabelvedere.it).

CHAPTER 3
TRANSPORTATION IN BOLOGNA

3.1 Getting to Bologna
Getting to Bologna is the first step in an unforgettable adventure. Here, we'll explore the various ways to reach this captivating city, providing all the details you need to plan your journey.

Arriving by Air
Flying to Bologna is often the most convenient option for international travelers. Bologna Guglielmo Marconi Airport (BLQ) is well-connected to major cities across Europe and beyond. Numerous airlines offer flights to Bologna, including budget carriers like Ryanair and easyJet, as well as full-service airlines such as Lufthansa, British Airways, and Air France. These airlines provide regular services, making it easy to find a flight that suits your schedule and budget. Here are some of the airlines that fly to Bologna, along with their websites:

-Ryanair: Known for its budget-friendly fares, Ryanair offers numerous flights to Bologna from various European cities. Their website is (https://www.ryanair.com).

-easyJet: Another budget airline, easyJet provides extensive service to Bologna from many European destinations. You can book tickets at (https://www.easyjet.com).

-Lufthansa: As Germany's flagship carrier, Lufthansa connects Bologna with several major cities across Europe and beyond. Their website is (https://www.lufthansa.com).

-British Airways: Offering a range of flights to Bologna, British Airways provides a comfortable travel experience from the UK and other locations. Visit (https://www.britishairways.com) for booking.

-Air France: Connecting Bologna to numerous international destinations, Air France is known for its service and reliability. Book flights at (https://www.airfrance.com).

Ticket prices for flights to Bologna can vary widely depending on the time of year, how far in advance you book, and the airline you choose. On average, a round-trip ticket from major European cities like London, Paris, or Frankfurt can range from €50 to €200 with budget airlines, while full-service airlines might charge between €150 and €400. Once you arrive at Bologna Airport, getting to the city center is straightforward. The Aerobus service connects the airport with Bologna Centrale, the main train station, in about 20 minutes. Tickets cost around €6 and can be purchased online or at the airport.

Traveling by Train

For those already in Europe, traveling to Bologna by train can be a scenic and comfortable alternative. Bologna Centrale is one of Italy's busiest railway hubs, with high-speed trains linking it to major cities like Milan, Florence, Rome, and Venice. Trenitalia and Italo are the primary train operators, offering frequent services and a range of ticket options to suit different budgets. High-speed trains, known as Frecciarossa and Italo, provide the fastest connections, with travel times of about one hour from Florence, two hours from Milan, and just under three hours from Rome. Ticket prices for these trains vary, with advance purchase fares starting as low as €20 for short journeys and up to €70 or more for longer trips. It is advisable to book tickets early, especially during peak travel seasons, to secure the best prices. Tickets can be purchased directly from the Trenitalia and Italo websites, which also offer information on schedules and seat availability.

-Trenitalia: The primary operator of Italy's national rail network, offering extensive routes and schedules. Their website is (https://www.trenitalia.com).

-Italo: A private high-speed train operator known for its modern trains and competitive prices. Book tickets at (https://www.italotreno.it).

For a more leisurely journey, regional trains are also available, offering a chance to see the Italian countryside. These trains are slower but often less expensive, with tickets that can be bought on the day of travel without significant price fluctuations.

Reaching Bologna by Road

Driving to Bologna is a viable option for those who enjoy road trips and the flexibility of having their own vehicle. The city is well-connected by Italy's extensive autostrada (highway) network, making it easily accessible from various parts of the country. The A1 motorway, known as the Autostrada del Sole, links Bologna to Milan in the north and Rome in the south. Additionally, the A14 motorway connects Bologna to the Adriatic coast. Driving in Italy requires a valid driver's license, and non-EU visitors should carry an International Driving Permit. Be aware of the ZTL (Zona a Traffico Limitato) zones in Bologna's city center, where vehicle access is restricted to reduce traffic congestion and pollution. Parking can also be challenging and expensive in central areas, so it's often best to use public parking facilities on the outskirts and rely on public transport to reach the city center.

3.1 Public Transport: Buses and Trains

The city's public transportation network is well-developed, offering residents and visitors a variety of options to navigate the city and its surroundings with ease. Whether traveling by bus, train, or other modes of transport, Bologna provides a seamless and cost-effective means to explore its many attractions and neighborhoods.

Buses in Bologna

The bus system in Bologna is operated by TPER (Trasporto Passeggeri Emilia-Romagna), providing extensive coverage across the city and surrounding areas. Buses are a primary mode of public transport in Bologna, with numerous routes that connect key points of interest, residential areas, and commercial hubs. The bus network operates from early morning until late at night, ensuring accessibility for commuters and tourists alike. Bus tickets in Bologna can be purchased at various locations, including ticket machines at bus stops, authorized retailers, and through mobile apps. A single bus ticket costs around €1.50 and is valid for 75 minutes, allowing unlimited transfers within this time frame. For those planning to use buses frequently, there are options for day passes, weekly passes, and monthly passes, offering significant savings. A day pass costs approximately €5, providing unlimited travel on buses for the entire day, while a monthly pass is priced around €36.

Trains in Bologna

Bologna's central location in Italy makes it a crucial railway hub, with its main train station, Bologna Centrale, being one of the busiest in the country. The train services in Bologna are managed by Trenitalia and Italo, two of the major train operators in Italy. Bologna Centrale connects the city with numerous national and international destinations, making train travel a convenient option for both short and long-distance journeys. The train system includes high-speed trains (Frecciarossa, Frecciargento, and Italo) that link Bologna with major cities like Milan, Florence, Rome, and Venice. Regional trains also operate frequently, providing connections to nearby towns and cities within the Emilia-Romagna region. Train tickets vary in price depending on the type of train and the distance traveled. For example, high-speed train tickets from Bologna to Florence can cost between €20 to €40, while regional train tickets for shorter distances are more affordable, typically ranging from €3 to €15.

Navigating Bologna with Public Transportation

Navigating Bologna using public transportation is straightforward, thanks to the city's well-integrated system and user-friendly services. Visitors can benefit from several tools and resources to plan their journeys effectively. TPER and Trenitalia websites, as well as their respective mobile apps, offer real-time information on routes, schedules, and ticket purchases. These platforms also provide interactive maps, making it easier to identify the best routes and connections. For tourists, Bologna Welcome, the city's official tourism portal, offers comprehensive information on public transportation options, including detailed guides and tips for getting around. Visitors can also take advantage of the Bologna Welcome Card, which includes free or discounted access to public transportation and various attractions, providing a convenient way to explore the city.

3.2 Biking in Bologna

Biking in Bologna is not only convenient but also an environmentally friendly way to explore. This comprehensive guide provides detailed insights into the biking systems, routes, rental options, and tips for visitors.

Biking Systems and Routes in Bologna

Bologna boasts an extensive network of bike paths that weave through its historical center and extend to its outskirts. The city's commitment to sustainable transportation is evident in its well-maintained cycling infrastructure, making it a haven for both casual cyclists and avid bikers.

Urban Cycling Routes

The historical center of Bologna, characterized by its iconic porticoes and medieval architecture, is ideal for urban cycling. Key routes include Via dell'Indipendenza, which leads to the central Piazza Maggiore, and Via Rizzoli, offering scenic views of the Two Towers, Asinelli and Garisenda. The well-marked bike lanes ensure a safe and enjoyable ride, allowing cyclists to effortlessly navigate through the city's bustling streets and quiet alleys.

Scenic and Recreational Routes

For those seeking a more leisurely ride, Bologna offers several scenic routes that highlight the city's natural beauty. The Bologna Hills, located just south of the city, provide a perfect escape with trails like the Parco di Villa Ghigi, offering panoramic views of the cityscape and surrounding countryside. The Reno River pathway is another popular route, stretching along the riverbanks and providing a serene environment for cycling.

Greenways and Parks

Bologna's greenways and parks, such as the Giardini Margherita, are perfect for family-friendly biking. These areas are designed for relaxation and outdoor activities, featuring wide paths suitable for cyclists of all ages. The Bicipolitana network, inspired by the concept of urban metros, connects various parks and green areas, making it easy to explore the city's natural spaces.

Bike Rental Companies

Bologna offers a variety of bike rental services catering to different needs and preferences. These companies provide a range of bicycles, from standard city bikes to electric bikes, ensuring that visitors can find the perfect ride for their adventure.

Dynamo Velostazione

Dynamo Velostazione, located near the Bologna Centrale railway station, is one of the most popular bike rental services in the city. It offers a wide selection of bicycles, including city bikes, mountain bikes, and e-bikes. Rental prices start at around €10 per day for a standard city bike, with additional options available for longer-term rentals. Dynamo Velostazione also provides guided bike tours, allowing visitors to explore Bologna with knowledgeable local guides. Website: (http://www.dynamobologna.it/).

Bi-Bo Bike Rental

Bi-Bo Bike Rental is another excellent option for visitors. Conveniently located in the city center, Bi-Bo offers competitive pricing, with daily rentals starting at approximately €12. Their fleet includes city bikes, children's bikes, and accessories such as helmets and child seats. Bi-Bo also provides maps and suggested routes, helping cyclists make the most of their biking experience in Bologna. Website: (https://www.bibobikerental.com/).

Ridemovi

Ridemovi is a bike-sharing service that operates throughout Bologna. This system is particularly convenient for short trips and spontaneous rides. Users can locate and unlock bikes via the Ridemovi app, with rental costs calculated based on duration. Prices typically range from €0.50 for 30 minutes to €5 for a full day. Ridemovi bikes are strategically placed around the city, making it easy to pick up and drop off bikes at various locations. Website: (https://www.ridemovi.it/).

Navigating Bologna by Bike

Effectively navigating Bologna by bike requires a bit of preparation and awareness of local biking etiquette. Here are some tips to ensure a smooth and enjoyable biking experience in the city.

Planning Your Route

Before setting out, it's beneficial to plan your route. Utilize maps and cycling apps to identify bike lanes, scenic routes, and points of interest. Bologna's Tourist Information Centers offer free maps highlighting bike paths and recommended cycling routes.

Understanding Traffic Rules

Bologna's traffic regulations for cyclists are similar to those in other European cities. Cyclists must adhere to traffic signals, ride in the direction of traffic, and use designated bike lanes where available. Wearing a helmet, while not mandatory, is strongly recommended for safety. Additionally, cyclists should equip their bikes with front and rear lights, especially when riding at night.

Bike Parking

Bologna provides numerous bike parking facilities, particularly around major attractions, transport hubs, and public spaces. It is advisable to use these designated areas to prevent theft and avoid fines. Secure your bike with a sturdy lock, and consider using multiple locks for added security.

Respecting Pedestrians

Bologna's historical center is often crowded with pedestrians, especially in popular areas like Piazza Maggiore and Via Zamboni. Cyclists should ride at a moderate speed, yield to pedestrians, and avoid cycling on sidewalks unless explicitly permitted.

Guided Tours and Group Rides

For those new to the city, joining a guided bike tour can be an excellent way to explore Bologna. These tours provide historical insights, highlight hidden gems, and ensure a safe and structured biking experience. Several companies, including Dynamo Velostazione and Bi-Bo Bike Rental, offer guided tours tailored to different interests and fitness levels.

3.3 Taxis and Ride-Sharing Services

Navigating this bustling city is made easier through a variety of transportation options, including taxis and ride-sharing services. These services are reliable, readily available, and cater to the diverse needs of tourists and residents alike.

Here's an in-depth look at some of the key taxi and ride-sharing services in Bologna, providing all the essential details a visitor might need.

Traditional Taxis in Bologna

Taxis in Bologna are a convenient way to travel, especially for those who prefer direct routes and personal service. The city's taxi fleet is modern and well-regulated, ensuring safety and comfort.

Cotabo Taxi

Cotabo is one of Bologna's largest and most reputable taxi cooperatives. With a fleet of well-maintained vehicles, Cotabo ensures reliable and efficient service throughout the city. They are located at Via Stalingrado, 61, Bologna. Visitors can book a Cotabo taxi through their website (http://www.cotabo.it/). Prices start at around €5 for the base fare, with additional charges based on distance and time.

Radiotaxi Cat

Radiotaxi Cat is another prominent taxi service in Bologna, known for its punctuality and customer-oriented approach. Their office is situated at Via di Saliceto, 4, Bologna. To book a ride, visitors can visit their website (http://www.catradiotaxi.it/). The fare structure includes a base rate of approximately €5, with costs increasing based on the distance traveled and time spent.

Taxi Bologna

Taxi Bologna offers a comprehensive taxi service with a focus on convenience and reliability. Their headquarters is located at Via Emilia Ponente, 30, Bologna. Customers can reach them through their website (https://www.taxibologna.it/). Pricing is competitive, starting at €5 for the initial fare, with incremental charges applied for distance and duration.

Ride-Sharing Services in Bologna

In addition to traditional taxis, ride-sharing services have become increasingly popular in Bologna. These services offer flexibility and ease of use, often accessed through mobile apps that make booking a ride straightforward and quick.

Uber

Uber, a globally recognized ride-sharing service, operates in Bologna, providing a seamless way to get around the city. Users can book a ride via the Uber app, which allows for various options such as UberX, UberBlack, and UberVan to suit different needs and group sizes. The fare for an Uber ride typically starts at around €1 per kilometer, with additional costs for time and demand.

Free Now

Free Now, formerly known as mytaxi, is another major player in Bologna's ride-sharing market. It offers an intuitive app-based booking system, allowing users to choose from a range of vehicles, including eco-friendly options. Free Now's headquarters in Bologna is at Via Mazzini, 10. Contact can be made through their website (https://www.free-now.com/). Pricing is competitive, starting with a base fare of approximately €3, with further charges based on distance and ride duration.

TaxiClick Easy

TaxiClick Easy is an innovative service that bridges traditional taxis and modern ride-sharing. Users can book taxis directly through the TaxiClick app, offering the convenience of ride-sharing with the reliability of traditional taxi services. Their office is located at Via delle Lame, 50, Bologna. More information can be found on their website (https://www.taxiclick.com/). The fare structure is similar to traditional taxis, with a base fare around €5 and incremental charges for distance and time.

Tips for Using Taxis and Ride-Sharing Services

When using taxis or ride-sharing services in Bologna, it is advisable to confirm the fare before starting your journey, especially during peak hours when demand might drive prices higher. Additionally, tipping is appreciated but not mandatory, typically rounding up to the nearest euro or adding a small amount for exceptional service.

Accessibility and Special Services

Many taxi and ride-sharing companies in Bologna offer accessible vehicles for passengers with mobility issues. It is recommended to specify any special requirements when booking to ensure the appropriate vehicle is dispatched.

3.4 Car Rentals and Driving Tips

Car rentals provide the freedom to travel at your leisure, making it easier to visit picturesque towns, scenic vineyards, and historical landmarks scattered across the countryside. Bologna hosts several reputable car rental companies, each offering a variety of vehicles and services to meet diverse travel needs.

Major Car Rental Companies in Bologna

In Bologna, several well-known car rental companies provide reliable services. Avis, Europcar, Hertz, Enterprise, and Sixt are some of the major names you will encounter. These companies typically have their main offices conveniently located near Bologna Centrale, the city's central train station, as well as at Bologna Guglielmo Marconi Airport.

Avis

Avis is one of the leading car rental companies with a prominent office at Bologna Centrale and another at the airport. Their address at the train station is Piazza delle Medaglie d'Oro, 4, and they can be reached at, www.avis.com, provides detailed information on available vehicles and rental rates. Avis offers a wide range of cars from compact city cars to larger family vehicles and luxury models. Prices start at approximately €25 per day for a compact car, though rates can vary based on the season and availability.

Europcar

Europcar maintains offices at Bologna Centrale and the airport, with the central office located at Via Amendola, 9/A. They can be contacted via phone at +39 051 243564, and their website, www.europcar.com, offers an easy online booking system. Europcar is known for its extensive fleet, including eco-friendly vehicles and premium cars. Rental prices typically begin at around €30 per day for a small car.

Hertz

Hertz operates from Via dell'Aeroporto, 84/86 at the Bologna Airport, and from the train station at Via Boldrini, 4. They can be reached at their website, www.hertz.com, provides comprehensive details on their fleet and services. Hertz is favored for its competitive pricing, with daily rates starting at approximately €28 for an economy car.

Enterprise

Enterprise is well-represented in Bologna with an office at Via del Triumvirato, 84, near the airport, and another near the central station. They can be contacted at their website, www.enterprise.com. Enterprise offers a variety of vehicles, from budget options to luxury cars, with prices starting at around €27 per day.

Sixt

Sixt is known for its premium fleet and excellent customer service, with an office at the Bologna Airport located at Via del Triumvirato, 84. They can be reached at their website, www.sixt.com. Sixt offers a range of vehicles, including high-end and luxury models, with rental rates beginning at approximately €35 per day.

Driving in Bologna

Driving in Bologna can be both an exciting and challenging experience, particularly for those unfamiliar with Italian driving customs and road regulations. The city's historic center is characterized by narrow streets and limited traffic zones (ZTL), which restrict vehicle access to reduce congestion and preserve the area's charm. It is essential to be aware of these zones, as unauthorized entry can result in substantial fines. Visitors can find detailed maps and guidelines regarding ZTL zones on the city's official website or through their car rental company.

Parking in Bologna

Parking in Bologna is another factor to consider. While there are numerous parking garages and lots available, finding street parking can be challenging, especially in the city center. Many hotels offer parking facilities, and it is advisable to confirm parking options when booking accommodations. The average cost for parking in a garage ranges from €2 to €3 per hour, with daily rates typically around €20.

Italy's Motorways and Road Regulations

Italy's motorways (autostrade) are well-maintained and connect Bologna to major cities and regions. These roads are toll-based, and it is recommended to carry some cash or a credit card for payment at toll booths. Speed limits on autostrade are generally 130 km/h (about 81 mph), while on secondary roads, limits vary between 50 km/h (31 mph) and 90 km/h (56 mph), depending on the area. It is crucial to adhere to these limits and be cautious of traffic cameras, which are prevalent throughout Italy.

CHAPTER 4
TOP 10 HIDDEN GEM ATTRACTIONS

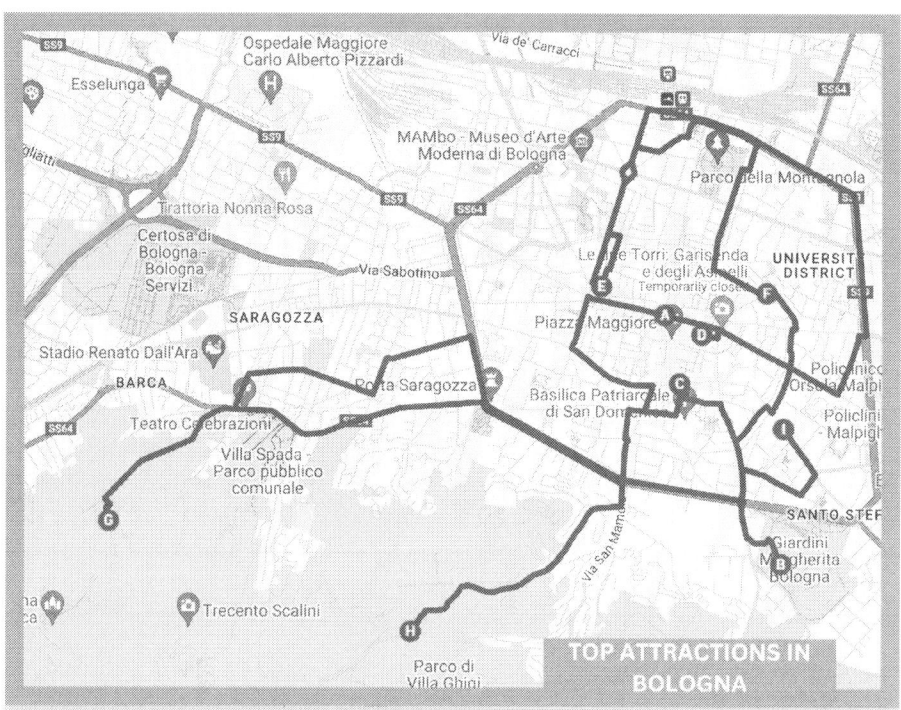

Directions from Bologna, Metropolitan City of Bologna, Italy to Complesso baraccano, Via Santo Stefano, Bologna, Metropolitan City of Bologna, Italy

A
Bologna, Metropolitan City of Bologna, Italy

D
Mercato di Mezzo, Via Clavature, Bologna, Metropolitan City of Bologna, Italy

G
Portico di San Luca, Bologna, Metropolitan City of Bologna, Italy

B
Giardini Margherita, Viale Giovanni Gozzadini, Bologna, Metropolitan City of Bologna, Italy

E
Mercato delle Erbe, Via Ugo Bassi, Bologna, Metropolitan City of Bologna, Italy

H
Villa Ghigi, Via San Mamolo, Bologna, Metropolitan City of Bologna, Italy

C
Biblioteca comunale dell'Archiginnasio, Piazza Galvani, Bologna, Metropolitan City of Bologna, Italy

F
Oratory of Santa Cecilia, Via Zamboni, Bologna, Metropolitan City of Bologna, Italy

I
Complesso baraccano, Via Santo Stefano, Bologna, Metropolitan City of Bologna, Italy

4.1 Santo Stefano Complex

The Santo Stefano Complex stands as a testament to the city's rich historical and architectural heritage. Known locally as "Sette Chiese" or "Seven Churches," this magnificent ensemble of religious buildings offers visitors a unique journey through centuries of history, art, and culture. Each corner of this complex holds a story waiting to be discovered, making it an essential visit for anyone exploring Bologna.

The Basilica of Santo Stefano

The Basilica of Santo Stefano, often referred to as the "Holy Jerusalem of Bologna," is the centerpiece of the complex. This ancient basilica, with its origins dating back to the 5th century, serves as a captivating introduction to the broader site. Located at Piazza Santo Stefano, it is easily accessible from the city center by a short walk or via public transportation, such as buses that stop at nearby Via Santo Stefano. The basilica itself is a marvel of early Christian architecture, characterized by its austere brick facade and the serene beauty of its interiors. Stepping inside, visitors are greeted by a dimly lit nave, where the air is filled with the scent of old wood and candle wax. The ambiance is one of profound tranquility, inviting quiet contemplation. The highlight within is the intricate mosaic floor, a relic of the church's earliest days, which provides a tangible connection to Bologna's ancient past.

The Courtyard of Pilate

Adjacent to the Basilica, the Courtyard of Pilate is another must-see feature of the Santo Stefano Complex. This charming courtyard is named after Pontius Pilate and is designed to resemble the courtyard of his house in Jerusalem, reflecting the complex's nickname. The courtyard is an open-air space surrounded by porticos, featuring a central fountain that symbolizes the biblical Basin of Pilate. Visitors can access the courtyard through the basilica or directly from the square. The Courtyard of Pilate is free to enter and is an ideal spot for those looking to immerse themselves in the serene ambiance of the complex. The historical and cultural significance of this courtyard is profound, as it is believed to have been part of a pilgrimage route for early Christians, replicating the holy sites of Jerusalem.

The Church of the Holy Sepulchre

Another jewel within the Santo Stefano Complex is the Church of the Holy Sepulchre. This church, modeled after the Church of the Holy Sepulchre in Jerusalem, is a fascinating blend of history and spirituality. To reach this church, one must navigate through the interconnected buildings of the complex, each transition offering a new perspective on the site's layered history. The Church of the Holy Sepulchre stands out for its octagonal shape, which is quite unique among the churches in Bologna. The central plan of the church is said to be inspired by the original church in Jerusalem, adding a layer of authenticity to the complex's biblical associations. Inside, the church houses a replica of the sepulcher of Christ, enhancing its significance as a pilgrimage site.

The Cloister of Santo Stefano

The Cloister of Santo Stefano is a hidden gem within the complex, offering a quiet retreat from the bustling city outside. This cloister, dating back to the 10th century, is an exquisite example of Romanesque architecture, with its harmonious proportions and elegant arches. The cloister can be accessed from within the complex, following signs that guide visitors through a labyrinth of ancient hallways. Walking through the cloister, visitors are enveloped in a sense of calm, accentuated by the gentle sound of water trickling from a central fountain. The well-maintained garden in the cloister is a delight, with blooming flowers and carefully trimmed bushes adding to the serene environment. The space is often used for temporary exhibitions, concerts, and cultural events, making each visit potentially unique.

The Museum of Santo Stefano

Completing the experience of the Santo Stefano Complex is the Museum of Santo Stefano. This museum is housed within the complex and offers a curated collection of religious artifacts, historical documents, and artworks that span the centuries. The museum is located near the entrance of the complex and can be easily found by following the informative signs. The museum provides a comprehensive overview of the history and significance of the Santo Stefano Complex. Exhibits include ancient manuscripts, liturgical objects, and stunning pieces of medieval art. Each artifact is carefully labeled with detailed descriptions, allowing visitors to gain a deeper understanding of the religious and cultural heritage of Bologna.

4.2 Basilica di San Domenico

Basilica di San Domenico stands out as a beacon of religious, artistic, and historical significance. Situated in the heart of Bologna, this basilica is not merely a place of worship but a treasure trove of art and history. For those planning to explore Bologna, here are top attractions within the Basilica di San Domenico that are must-see highlights, each offering a unique glimpse into the city's profound heritage.

The Tomb of Saint Dominic

The Tomb of Saint Dominic is undoubtedly one of the most compelling attractions within the basilica. Located in the chapel dedicated to him, the tomb is an exquisite piece of art that commands attention. The intricate design and craftsmanship are attributed to the collaboration of several renowned artists, including Nicola Pisano, Arnolfo di Cambio, and Michelangelo Buonarroti, who contributed to the tomb's final form. To visit the tomb, head to the Basilica di San Domenico at Piazza San Domenico. It's a short walk from the city center, making it easily accessible by foot. There is no entry fee to visit the basilica, although donations are appreciated. The tomb's historical significance is immense, as it houses the remains of Saint Dominic, the founder of the Dominican Order, who passed away in 1221. His life and work had a profound impact on the Catholic Church, and this site is a pilgrimage destination for many.

The Ark of Saint Dominic

Another remarkable attraction is the Ark of Saint Dominic, a stunning monument that encases the saint's relics. This marble sarcophagus, located within the basilica, is a marvel of Gothic art. The Ark is embellished with intricate sculptures depicting scenes from the life of Saint Dominic and other biblical narratives, making it a significant piece for both art historians and religious devotees. Visitors can find the Ark in the main chapel of the basilica, a testament to the collaborative efforts of several artists over many years. The most famous contributor is Michelangelo, who sculpted three statues for the Ark during his early career. His works, including the statues of Saint Petronius, Saint Proculus, and an angel holding a candlestick, are highlights that draw art enthusiasts from around the globe.

The Rosary Chapel

The Rosary Chapel, also known as the Chapel of the Madonna of the Rosary, is another must-see within the Basilica di San Domenico. This chapel is renowned for its stunning Baroque architecture and decoration, which stand in contrast to the Gothic elements found elsewhere in the basilica. Located on the right side of the basilica's nave, the Rosary Chapel is easily accessible to all visitors. The chapel is free to enter, though donations are encouraged to help maintain its beauty. The Rosary Chapel is a vibrant display of religious art, featuring paintings and frescoes that depict the mysteries of the Rosary and the life of the Virgin Mary.

The Choir Stalls

The Choir Stalls in the Basilica di San Domenico are a hidden gem that should not be missed. These wooden stalls, located in the choir area behind the main altar, are masterpieces of Renaissance woodworking. Crafted in the 16th century by the renowned woodcarver Damiano da Bergamo, the stalls feature intricate intarsia work depicting scenes from the Old and New Testaments. To reach the choir area, visitors can follow the signs within the basilica. Access to the choir stalls is included with general admission, which remains donation-based. The historical significance of the choir stalls lies in their artistic and liturgical functions. They were used by the Dominican friars during their daily prayers and are a testament to the blend of functionality and beauty in Renaissance art.

The Cloisters

The Cloisters of the Basilica di San Domenico provide a peaceful retreat within the bustling city of Bologna. These cloisters, which include the Old and the New Cloister, are serene spaces that offer a glimpse into the monastic life of the Dominican friars. The Old Cloister dates back to the 13th century, while the New Cloister was added in the 16th century. The cloisters can be accessed from within the basilica and are open to visitors for free, though donations are always welcome. The cloisters are historically significant as they have been a part of the Dominican convent since its foundation. They offer a tranquil environment for reflection and a chance to admire the architectural evolution over centuries.

4.3 Giardini Margherita

In the heart of Bologna lies a verdant oasis known as Giardini Margherita, a quintessential Italian park that offers a respite from the city's bustling streets. This enchanting green space, named after Queen Margherita of Savoy, is not just a park; it's a cultural hub, a historical landmark, and a recreational haven rolled into one.

Exploring the Park

Upon entering Giardini Margherita, visitors are greeted by lush greenery, tranquil lakes, and winding pathways that beckon exploration. Whether you're seeking a leisurely stroll, a picnic with friends, or a romantic boat ride on the lake, the park offers something for everyone. Admire the vibrant floral displays in the botanical garden, challenge your friends to a game of tennis or volleyball, or simply relax on the grassy lawns and soak up the sun.

Cultural Attractions

In addition to its natural beauty, Giardini Margherita boasts several cultural attractions that showcase Bologna's rich heritage. One such highlight is the historic Casina del Ghiaccio, a charming ice-skating rink housed in a 19th-century building. Here, visitors can glide across the ice amidst stunning architectural surroundings, making for a memorable experience.

Culinary Delights

No visit to Giardini Margherita would be complete without sampling the culinary delights on offer. The park is home to numerous cafes and restaurants where visitors can savor traditional Italian cuisine, from freshly baked pizzas to decadent gelato. Whether you're craving a quick espresso or a leisurely meal overlooking the lake, the park's dining options cater to every palate.

Family-Friendly Activities

Giardini Margherita is the perfect destination for families seeking a day of fun and adventure. Children can unleash their energy at the park's playgrounds, which feature swings, slides, and climbing frames suitable for kids of all ages. Additionally, the park hosts regular events and workshops tailored to young visitors, ensuring that there's never a dull moment for families exploring its grounds.

4.4 Archiginnasio of Bologna

This magnificent building, originally constructed in the 16th century to house the University of Bologna, is now a top attraction for visitors seeking to delve into the city's intellectual past. With its stunning architecture, historical significance, and wealth of cultural treasures, the Archiginnasio offers a captivating journey through time.

The Anatomy Theatre

One of the most intriguing features of the Archiginnasio is the Anatomy Theatre, a unique and meticulously preserved space where medical students once observed dissections. Located on the ground floor of the building, the Anatomy Theatre is easily accessible from the main entrance on Piazza Galvani. Visitors can reach the Archiginnasio on foot from various points in the city center, or by public transportation, with several bus stops nearby.

The Teatro Anatomico

Adjacent to the Anatomy Theatre is the Teatro Anatomico, another must-see attraction within the Archiginnasio. This ornate lecture hall, adorned with elaborate frescoes and intricate carvings, served as the venue for academic lectures and ceremonies. Accessible through the same entrance as the Anatomy

Theatre, the Teatro Anatomico offers visitors a glimpse into the intellectual life of Renaissance Bologna.

The Archiginnasio Library

No visit to the Archiginnasio would be complete without a stop at the Archiginnasio Library, home to one of the most extensive collections of rare books and manuscripts in Italy. Located on the upper floors of the building, the library is accessible via a majestic staircase adorned with marble balustrades and allegorical statues. Visitors can reach the library by climbing the stairs from the main entrance hall. The Archiginnasio Library holds immense historical and cultural significance as a repository of Bologna's intellectual heritage. Many of the books and manuscripts housed here are rare or unique, offering invaluable insights into the history of scholarship in Italy and beyond.

The Stabat Mater Hall

Another highlight of the Archiginnasio is the Stabat Mater Hall, a magnificent space adorned with stunning frescoes and intricate stucco decorations. This grand hall, located on the upper floors of the building, was once used for academic ceremonies and official functions. Accessible via the same staircase as the library, the Stabat Mater Hall offers visitors a glimpse into the opulent surroundings of Renaissance academia. The Stabat Mater Hall holds significant historical and cultural importance as a symbol of Bologna's intellectual prestige during the Renaissance. It was here that scholars and dignitaries gathered to celebrate academic achievements and discuss the pressing issues of the day. Today, visitors can experience the same sense of grandeur and intellectual fervor as they explore this magnificent hall.

4.5 Museum of Modern Art of Bologna (MAMbo)

The Museum of Modern Art of Bologna (MAMbo) stands as a beacon of contemporary artistic expression in the city. Established in 2007, MAMbo has quickly risen to prominence as a must-visit destination for art enthusiasts and cultural aficionados alike. With its diverse collection, dynamic exhibitions, and innovative programming, MAMbo offers visitors a unique opportunity to engage with the vibrant world of modern and contemporary art.

The Permanent Collection

One of the highlights of MAMbo is its impressive permanent collection, which spans the breadth of modern and contemporary art movements. Located on the museum's upper floors, the permanent collection features works by renowned artists such as Giorgio Morandi, Lucio Fontana, and Alberto Burri, among others. From abstract expressionism to conceptual art, the collection offers a comprehensive overview of the evolution of artistic styles and techniques over the past century. To explore the permanent collection, visitors can make their way to MAMbo, conveniently located at Via Don Giovanni Minzoni 14. The museum is easily accessible by public transportation, with several bus stops and train stations nearby. Admission fees vary depending on exhibitions and events, but general admission to the permanent collection is typically affordable, making it accessible to a wide range of visitors.

Temporary Exhibitions

In addition to its permanent collection, MAMbo hosts a diverse array of temporary exhibitions throughout the year, showcasing the work of both local and international artists. These exhibitions cover a wide range of themes and mediums, from painting and sculpture to video art and installation. Each exhibition offers a unique perspective on contemporary issues and challenges, inviting visitors to engage critically with the world around them. To stay updated on upcoming exhibitions and events, visitors can check MAMbo's website or follow them on social media. Entry fees for temporary exhibitions may vary, but many offer discounted or free admission for students and other groups. Whether you're interested in exploring cutting-edge installations or discovering emerging talents, MAMbo's temporary exhibitions promise to inspire and provoke thought.

Educational Programs and Workshops

In addition to its exhibitions, MAMbo offers a variety of educational programs and workshops designed to engage visitors of all ages. From guided tours and artist talks to hands-on art-making activities, these programs provide opportunities for learning, creativity, and discovery. Whether you're a seasoned art enthusiast or a curious beginner, there's something for everyone at MAMbo. Visitors interested in participating in educational programs can inquire at the museum's reception desk or check the website for upcoming events. While some programs may require advance registration or an additional fee, many are free and open to the public. By fostering a culture of lifelong learning and creativity, MAMbo seeks to empower individuals to connect with art in meaningful and transformative ways.

The Museum Cafe and Shop

After immersing yourself in the world of contemporary art, take some time to relax and unwind at MAMbo's cafe. Located within the museum, the cafe offers a cozy atmosphere where visitors can enjoy a refreshing drink or a delicious meal. Whether you're looking for a quick snack or a leisurely lunch, the cafe is the perfect place to refuel and reflect on your museum experience. In addition to the cafe, MAMbo also boasts a well-stocked museum shop where visitors can purchase unique souvenirs and gifts. From art books and posters to jewelry and home decor, the shop offers a curated selection of items inspired by the museum's collection and exhibitions. Whether you're shopping for yourself or searching for the perfect gift, you're sure to find something special at MAMbo's museum shop.

4.6 Bologna Food Markets: Mercato di Mezzo, Mercato delle Erbe

Bologna's culinary scene are its vibrant food markets, each offering a sensory journey through the region's rich gastronomic heritage. From Mercato di Mezzo to Mercato delle Erbe, these bustling markets are a must-visit for anyone seeking an authentic taste of Bologna.

Mercato di Mezzo

Located in the city center, Mercato di Mezzo is a historic market dating back to the Middle Ages. Nestled amidst narrow cobblestone streets, this charming market is a food lover's paradise, brimming with an array of local delicacies and traditional products. To reach Mercato di Mezzo, visitors can easily walk from

Piazza Maggiore, the main square of Bologna, or take public transportation to nearby stops.

Mercato delle Erbe

Another iconic food market in Bologna is Mercato delle Erbe, situated just a short distance from the city center. Housed in a historic building dating back to the 19th century, this bustling market is a favorite among locals and tourists alike. To reach Mercato delle Erbe, visitors can take a leisurely stroll from Piazza Maggiore or hop on a bus to nearby stops. Similar to Mercato di Mezzo, Mercato delle Erbe does not charge an entry fee, allowing visitors to explore its offerings at their leisure. Its cultural significance lies in its status as a hub of Bolognese cuisine, where traditional recipes and culinary techniques have been passed down through generations.

La Piazzola Market

For those seeking a more off-the-beaten-path experience, La Piazzola Market offers a unique glimpse into Bologna's culinary scene. Located in the Santo Stefano district, this lively market is known for its eclectic mix of vendors selling a diverse array of products. To reach La Piazzola Market, visitors can take a scenic walk from the city center or hop on a bus to nearby stops. As with the other markets, there is no entry fee to visit La Piazzola Market, making it an affordable destination for food enthusiasts of all budgets. Its historical significance lies in its role as a traditional neighborhood market, where locals come to stock up on fresh ingredients and socialize with their neighbors.

4.7 Oratory of Santa Cecilia

Oratory of Santa Cecilia stands as a hidden gem, offering visitors a glimpse into the city's rich religious and artistic heritage. This small yet remarkable oratory, dedicated to the patron saint of music, is a must-see attraction for anyone exploring Bologna's cultural treasures. With its exquisite frescoes, stunning architecture, and serene ambiance, the Oratory of Santa Cecilia promises a memorable experience for visitors of all ages.

The Frescoes of Ludovico Carracci

One of the main draws of the Oratory of Santa Cecilia is its collection of frescoes by the renowned Baroque painter Ludovico Carracci. Located on the walls and ceiling of the oratory, these masterful artworks depict scenes from the life of Saint Cecilia, as well as other biblical and allegorical subjects. The frescoes are a testament to Carracci's talent and skill, showcasing his mastery of composition, color, and emotion. The frescoes of Ludovico Carracci hold immense historical and cultural significance, representing a pinnacle of Baroque art in Bologna. They offer valuable insights into the religious beliefs and artistic techniques of the period, providing a window into the cultural life of Renaissance Italy. Visitors can spend hours admiring the intricate details of the frescoes, each brushstroke telling a story of faith and creativity.

The Chapel of Saint Cecilia

At the heart of the Oratory of Santa Cecilia lies the Chapel of Saint Cecilia, a sacred space dedicated to the patron saint of music. This intimate chapel, adorned with marble columns and ornate decorations, exudes a sense of peace and serenity. Visitors can enter the chapel through a small doorway, leaving behind the hustle and bustle of the outside world to immerse themselves in quiet contemplation. The Chapel of Saint Cecilia is a place of pilgrimage for music lovers and devotees alike, offering a sanctuary for prayer and reflection. Visitors can pay their respects to the saint and offer prayers for inspiration and guidance. The chapel's atmosphere is conducive to meditation, with soft lighting and gentle music creating a sense of harmony and tranquility.

The Crypt of Santa Cecilia

Beneath the main altar of the Oratory of Santa Cecilia lies the Crypt of Santa Cecilia, a sacred space steeped in history and legend. This underground chamber is said to contain the remains of Saint Cecilia herself, making it a place of pilgrimage for believers seeking a connection to the saint. Visitors can descend into the crypt via a staircase located near the entrance of the oratory. Entry to the crypt is typically included in the same ticket as the oratory, although access may be restricted at certain times for religious ceremonies. The crypt itself is a simple yet profound space, with stone walls and flickering candlelight creating an atmosphere of reverence and awe. Visitors can pay their respects to the saint and offer prayers for her intercession.

The Chapel of the Holy Sacrament

Another highlight of the Oratory of Santa Cecilia is the Chapel of the Holy Sacrament, a small yet exquisite space dedicated to the Eucharist. This chapel,

located near the entrance of the oratory, is adorned with beautiful frescoes and religious icons, creating a sense of holiness and sanctity. Visitors can enter the chapel and spend a moment in quiet prayer and reflection.

4.8 Portico di San Luca

Portico di San Luca stands as a testament to the city's rich history and architectural splendor. This iconic portico, stretching over 3.5 kilometers, is not only a marvel of engineering but also a symbol of religious devotion and cultural heritage. For visitors to Bologna, a stroll along the Portico di San Luca is a must-do experience, offering panoramic views of the city and a journey through centuries of history and tradition.

The Portico Walk

The Portico di San Luca begins near the city center at the Porta Saragozza, a historic gate that once marked the entrance to Bologna. From there, visitors can embark on a leisurely walk along the portico, ascending gradually into the hills towards the Sanctuary of the Madonna di San Luca. The walk takes approximately 1-2 hours, depending on your pace, and offers breathtaking views of Bologna and the surrounding countryside along the way.

Sanctuary of the Madonna di San Luca

At the end of the portico lies the Sanctuary of the Madonna di San Luca, a magnificent basilica perched atop the Colle della Guardia hill. The sanctuary, with its distinctive red dome and towering portico, is a sight to behold, drawing visitors from near and far. Inside, visitors can marvel at the ornate Baroque interiors and pay homage to the miraculous icon of the Madonna di San Luca, which has been venerated for centuries. To reach the sanctuary, visitors can continue along the portico or take the convenient shuttle bus from Piazza Maggiore in the city center. Entry to the sanctuary is free, though donations are appreciated to support its upkeep and maintenance. Whether you're seeking spiritual solace or simply admiring the architectural beauty, a visit to the Sanctuary of the Madonna di San Luca is sure to leave a lasting impression.

Panoramic Views

One of the highlights of the Portico di San Luca is the panoramic views it offers of Bologna and the surrounding countryside. As you ascend the hill, you'll be treated to sweeping vistas of the city skyline, with its iconic red rooftops and medieval towers stretching out before you. On clear days, you can even see as far as the Apennine Mountains in the distance, adding to the sense of awe and wonder. Be sure to bring your camera along to capture the breathtaking scenery, especially as the sun sets over the city, bathing it in a warm golden light. The Portico di San Luca offers countless opportunities for memorable photographs, whether you're capturing the architectural details of the portico itself or the stunning vistas that unfold before you.

4.9 Villa Ghigi Park

Villa Ghigi Park, an enchanting green oasis that beckons visitors with its serene beauty and captivating charm. This sprawling park, named after the prominent Ghigi family who once owned the estate, is a must-visit destination for nature enthusiasts, history buffs, and anyone seeking a peaceful escape from the city's hustle and bustle.

Nature and Recreation

One of the highlights of Villa Ghigi Park is its abundant natural beauty, which provides a sanctuary for flora and fauna alike. The park is home to a diverse array of plant species, including towering trees, vibrant flowers, and fragrant herbs, making it a paradise for botany enthusiasts and amateur photographers. In addition to its natural wonders, Villa Ghigi Park offers a variety of recreational activities for visitors to enjoy. Whether you're looking to go for a leisurely stroll, have a picnic amidst the scenic surroundings, or simply relax and unwind in nature's embrace, the park provides ample opportunities for outdoor enjoyment.

Panoramic Views

One of the most captivating aspects of Villa Ghigi Park is its panoramic views of the surrounding countryside and the city of Bologna. From various vantage points within the park, visitors can enjoy sweeping vistas that stretch as far as the eye can see, offering a breathtaking perspective of the landscape below.

Cultural Events and Activities

Throughout the year, Villa Ghigi Park plays host to a variety of cultural events and activities that showcase the best of Bologna's arts and entertainment scene. From outdoor concerts and theater performances to art exhibitions and festivals, there's always something happening in the park to delight and inspire visitors of all ages.

4.10 Bologna Canals and Bridges

Exploring the Bologna Canals and Bridges is a must for any visitor seeking to uncover the hidden gems of this historic city. From leisurely strolls along the water's edge to admiring the architectural marvels that span its canals, there is much to discover and appreciate in this enchanting corner of Bologna.

Piazza Maggiore

Located at the heart of Bologna, Piazza Maggiore is the city's main square and a hub of activity. Surrounded by historic buildings such as the Palazzo d'Accursio, the Basilica of San Petronio, and the Palazzo dei Notai, the square is a magnificent showcase of Bologna's rich architectural heritage. Visitors can stroll around the square, marvel at the stunning facades, and soak in the vibrant atmosphere of this bustling gathering place.

Two Towers (Due Torri)

The Two Towers, namely the Asinelli Tower and the Garisenda Tower, are iconic symbols of Bologna's skyline. Dating back to the 12th century, these towering structures offer panoramic views of the city and its surroundings. Climbing the 498 steps to the top of the Asinelli Tower is a memorable experience, providing unparalleled vistas of Bologna's medieval streets and historic landmarks.

Archiginnasio of Bologna

The Archiginnasio is a magnificent Renaissance building that once housed the University of Bologna, the oldest university in the world. Its stunning architecture, adorned with intricate carvings and frescoes, makes it a must-see attraction for visitors. Highlights include the Anatomy Theatre, the Teatro Anatomico, and the Archiginnasio Library, which boasts a vast collection of rare books and manuscripts.

Basilica of Santo Stefano

Often referred to as the "Seven Churches," the Basilica of Santo Stefano is a unique complex of religious buildings dating back to the 5th century. Stepping inside, visitors are greeted by a serene atmosphere and architectural wonders such as the Courtyard of Pilate and the Church of the Holy Sepulchre. The basilica's rich history and spiritual significance make it a captivating destination for travelers.

Bologna Canals and Bridges

Although lesser-known than its Venetian counterpart, Bologna boasts a network of charming canals and picturesque bridges that add a touch of romance to the cityscape. Visitors can explore these hidden gems on foot or by boat, admiring the historic architecture and tranquil waters that wind their way through the city center. The Bologna Canals and Bridges offer a peaceful retreat from the hustle and bustle of urban life, making them a top attraction for visitors seeking a more intimate glimpse of the city's beauty.

4.11 Sports, Outdoor Activities and Adventures

Bologna offers a plethora of opportunities for sports enthusiasts and outdoor adventurers alike. From adrenaline-pumping activities to leisurely pursuits, the city and its surrounding countryside provide endless options for exploration and excitement.

Climbing in the Apennines

Located just a stone's throw from Bologna, the Apennine Mountains offer an ideal setting for rock climbing enthusiasts seeking a thrilling adventure. With its rugged terrain and scenic vistas, this majestic mountain range provides countless opportunities for climbers of all skill levels to test their mettle against nature's challenges. Several local companies offer guided climbing tours and instruction for beginners, as well as advanced expeditions for experienced climbers. Prices for tours vary depending on the duration and level of difficulty, but typically range from €50 to €150 per person. Special services may include equipment rental, transportation to and from the climbing site, and personalized instruction from certified guides. For more information and bookings, visitors can visit the official website of Bologna Climbing Adventures at www.bolognaclimbingadventures.com.

Cycling in the Bologna Hills

For those who prefer to explore on two wheels, cycling in the Bologna hills offers a thrilling way to experience the region's stunning scenery and charming villages. With its network of scenic trails and winding country roads, the countryside surrounding Bologna is a cyclist's paradise, offering opportunities for both leisurely rides and challenging ascents. Several local tour operators offer guided cycling tours of the Bologna hills, catering to cyclists of all abilities. Prices for tours vary depending on the duration and level of support provided, but typically range from €30 to €100 per person. Special services may include bike rental, helmet hire, and support vehicles for longer rides. For more information and bookings, visitors can visit the official website of Bologna Cycling Tours at www.bolognacyclingtours.com.

Paragliding in the Emilia-Romagna Sky

For thrill-seekers with a taste for adventure, paragliding in the skies above Emilia-Romagna offers an unforgettable experience. With its panoramic views and exhilarating flights, the region's diverse landscape provides the perfect backdrop for soaring high above the earth. Several local paragliding schools offer tandem flights and instruction for beginners, as well as advanced courses for those looking to hone their skills. Prices for tandem flights typically range from €100 to €200 per person, depending on the duration and altitude of the flight. Special services may include transportation to the launch site, equipment rental, and in-flight photography. For more information and bookings, visitors can visit the official website of Emilia-Romagna Paragliding Adventures at www.emiliaromagnaparagliding.com.

Hiking in the Regional Parks

For nature lovers and outdoor enthusiasts, hiking in the regional parks surrounding Bologna offers a chance to explore some of Italy's most stunning natural landscapes. From the lush forests of the Parco dei Gessi Bolognesi to the rugged peaks of the Parco Regionale dell'Abbazia di Monteveglio, the region boasts a diverse array of trails and terrain to suit every preference. Several local tour companies offer guided hiking tours of the regional parks, catering to hikers of all abilities. Prices for tours vary depending on the duration and difficulty of the hike, but typically range from €20 to €50 per person. Special services may include transportation to and from the trailhead, expert guides, and packed lunches. For more information and bookings, visitors can visit the official website of Bologna Hiking Adventures at www.bolognahikingadventures.com.

Kayaking on the Reno River

For water sports enthusiasts, kayaking on the Reno River offers a unique opportunity to explore Bologna's scenic waterways and picturesque landscapes. With its gentle currents and tranquil stretches, the river provides an ideal setting for paddlers of all skill levels to enjoy a day on the water.

Several local outfitters offer guided kayaking tours of the Reno River, providing everything from equipment rental to expert instruction. Prices for tours vary depending on the duration and distance of the paddle, but typically range from €30 to €80 per person. Special services may include transportation to and from the river, safety equipment, and snacks. For more information and bookings, visitors can visit the official website of Bologna Kayaking Adventures at www.bolognakayakingadventures.com.

4.12 Recommended Tour Operators and Guided Tours

Exploring the vibrant city of Bologna is an adventure filled with history, culture, and gastronomy waiting to be discovered. While wandering the cobblestone streets and medieval squares on your own can be enchanting, embarking on a guided tour with a knowledgeable local expert can elevate your experience to new heights. In Bologna, there are several reputable tour operators and guided tour options to choose from, each offering unique insights and experiences tailored to different interests and preferences.

Bologna Welcome Tours

Bologna Welcome Tours is a highly regarded tour operator located in the heart of the city, offering a wide range of guided tours and experiences to suit every traveler's needs. From walking tours of the historic center to culinary adventures and day trips to nearby attractions, Bologna Welcome Tours provides expert guides who are passionate about sharing their knowledge and love for the city. Prices for tours with Bologna Welcome Tours vary depending on the duration and type of experience, with options available for every budget. One unique feature of Bologna Welcome Tours is their emphasis on sustainable and responsible tourism, ensuring that their activities have a positive impact on the local community and environment. For more information and to book your tour, visit the official website of Bologna Welcome Tours: (https://www.bolognawelcome.com/en/home/).

Bologna Food Experience

For culinary enthusiasts eager to sample Bologna's world-renowned cuisine, Bologna Food Experience offers a range of mouthwatering food tours and cooking classes led by local experts. From traditional pasta-making workshops to gourmet food tours of the city's markets and eateries, Bologna Food Experience provides an immersive journey into the flavors and traditions of Emilian cuisine. Prices for tours with Bologna Food Experience vary depending on the duration and inclusions, with options available for individuals, couples, and groups. One special service offered by Bologna Food Experience is their personalized approach, allowing visitors to customize their food tour experience according to their preferences and dietary restrictions. For more information and to book your culinary adventure, visit the official website of Bologna Food Experience: (https://www.bolognafoodexperience.com/).

Discover Bologna

Discover Bologna is a reputable tour operator specializing in cultural and historical guided tours of the city's most iconic landmarks and hidden gems. Led by passionate local guides, Discover Bologna offers insightful walking tours of the historic center, visits to art galleries and museums, and themed tours focusing on specific aspects of Bologna's rich heritage. Prices for tours with Discover Bologna are competitive, with options available for private and group tours. One unique feature of Discover Bologna is their focus on storytelling, bringing the city's history and culture to life through engaging narratives and anecdotes that captivate visitors of all ages. For more information and to book your guided tour, visit the official website of Discover Bologna: (https://www.discoverbologna.it/).

Bologna Bike Tour

For those seeking a more active and eco-friendly way to explore Bologna, Bologna Bike Tour offers guided bicycle tours of the city and its surroundings. Led by experienced cyclists, these tours take participants on a scenic journey through Bologna's streets, parks, and historic sites, providing a unique perspective on the city's architecture and urban landscape. One special service offered by Bologna Bike Tour is their commitment to safety, providing well-maintained bicycles and helmets, as well as knowledgeable guides who ensure a fun and enjoyable experience for all participants. For more information and to book your bike tour, visit the official website of Bologna Bike Tour: (https://www.bolognabiketour.com/).

Italian Days Food Experience

Italian Days Food Experience offers immersive culinary tours and cooking classes that showcase the gastronomic delights of Bologna and the surrounding Emilia-Romagna region. Led by passionate food experts, these tours take participants on a journey to local farms, markets, and artisanal producers, where they can taste authentic Italian flavors and learn about traditional food production methods. One unique feature of Italian Days Food Experience is their focus on authenticity, partnering with small-scale producers and family-run businesses to offer an intimate and genuine culinary experience. For more information and to book your food tour, visit the official website of Italian Days Food Experience:(https://www.italiandays.it/).

CHAPTER 5
PRACTICAL INFORMATION AND TRAVEL RESOURCES

Scan the QR code with a device to view a comprehensive and larger map of Bologna

5.1 Maps and Navigation

In Bologna, both traditional paper maps and modern digital maps are available to guide you through the city's treasures. This guide provides an extensive overview of how to access these maps, ensuring you have all the information you need to explore Bologna with ease.

Bologna Tourist Map

For many travelers, there is something special about unfolding a paper map and plotting your course through a new city. Bologna offers a variety of tourist maps that can be easily obtained upon arrival. These maps are typically available at tourist information centers, hotels, and major transportation hubs such as the Bologna Centrale train station and the Bologna Guglielmo Marconi Airport. The paper maps of Bologna are detailed and user-friendly, highlighting key attractions like Piazza Maggiore, the Two Towers (Le Due Torri), and the Basilica di San Petronio. They often include helpful information about public transportation routes, pedestrian zones, and points of interest. Using a paper map allows for a tactile and engaging way to navigate the city, perfect for those who prefer a more traditional approach to exploration.

Digital Maps

Bologna's digital maps are accessible through various platforms, providing real-time updates and interactive capabilities that enhance the visitor experience. Popular digital map services like Google Maps and Apple Maps offer comprehensive coverage of Bologna, including street views, public transportation options, and walking directions. To access Bologna's digital maps, simply open your preferred map application on your smartphone or tablet. These maps allow you to search for specific locations, find the best routes, and even get recommendations for nearby restaurants and attractions. Additionally, digital maps can be invaluable for discovering hidden gems in Bologna that might not be highlighted on traditional paper maps.

Offline Access

One common concern for travelers is how to navigate a foreign city without relying on constant internet access. Fortunately, there are several ways to access Bologna's maps offline. Many digital map applications, such as Google Maps, offer the option to download maps for offline use. Before embarking on your adventure, simply download the map of Bologna to your device, ensuring you have access to navigation even when you don't have an internet connection. For those who prefer paper maps but want the benefits of digital technology, consider using a QR code. By scanning the QR code provided in this guide, you can quickly access a comprehensive map of Bologna. This feature combines the reliability of a paper map with the convenience of digital access, ensuring you are always prepared to explore the city.

5.2 Five Days Itinerary

Upon arriving in Bologna, visitors should take the time to settle into their accommodation. Whether staying in a charming boutique hotel in the historic center or a modern hotel near the train station, choosing the right base is crucial for a comfortable stay. Once settled, the first day should be dedicated to getting acquainted with the city. Begin with a leisurely stroll through the heart of Bologna, starting at Piazza Maggiore, the city's central square. This historic piazza is surrounded by iconic landmarks such as the Basilica di San Petronio, Palazzo dei Notai, and Palazzo d'Accursio. The square offers a perfect introduction to Bologna's architectural grandeur and vibrant atmosphere. From Piazza Maggiore, wander through the narrow, medieval streets of the Quadrilatero district, famous for its bustling markets and gourmet shops. This area is a paradise for food lovers, offering a tantalizing array of local products like cheese, cured meats, and fresh pasta. Enjoy a light lunch at one of the traditional trattorias, sampling Bolognese specialties such as tagliatelle al ragù or tortellini in brodo.

In the afternoon, visit the Archiginnasio, the first seat of the University of Bologna, which is the oldest university in the Western world. The building now houses the Municipal Library and the Anatomical Theatre, a stunning example of 17th-century architecture used for teaching anatomy. This visit provides a fascinating insight into Bologna's academic heritage and intellectual history. As evening approaches, head back to Piazza Maggiore where you can relax at an outdoor café, soaking in the lively atmosphere. Dinner can be enjoyed at a nearby restaurant, where visitors can savor more of Bologna's renowned cuisine, paired with a glass of local wine.

Day Two: Historical and Cultural Immersion

The second day in Bologna should be dedicated to exploring its rich history and cultural offerings. Begin with a visit to the Two Towers, the Asinelli and the Garisenda, which are among the city's most famous landmarks. Climbing the Asinelli Tower, the taller of the two, offers breathtaking views of Bologna's red-tiled rooftops and surrounding countryside. This experience is both exhilarating and educational, providing a panoramic perspective of the city's layout. Next, make your way to the Basilica di San Domenico, a significant religious site housing the remains of Saint Dominic, the founder of the Dominican Order. The basilica is renowned for its exquisite chapels and the Arca di San Domenico, a marble tomb adorned with sculptures by renowned artists including Michelangelo. For lunch, consider visiting the Mercato di Mezzo, a historic market offering a variety of food stalls and eateries. Here, visitors can sample an assortment of Italian delicacies and enjoy the lively market atmosphere.

In the afternoon, the focus should shift to Bologna's artistic heritage with a visit to the Pinacoteca Nazionale di Bologna. This national art gallery houses an impressive collection of works from the 13th to the 18th centuries, featuring masterpieces by artists such as Raphael, Titian, and the Carracci brothers. The gallery provides a comprehensive overview of Bologna's contribution to the art world and is a must-visit for art enthusiasts. As the day winds down, consider exploring the vibrant university district. This area is full of cafés, bars, and bookstores, reflecting the youthful energy of the city's student population. Enjoy dinner at a local restaurant, experiencing Bologna's nightlife and culinary delights in this dynamic part of the city.

Day Three: Culinary Adventures and Local Experiences
The third day should be dedicated to delving deeper into Bologna's world-famous culinary scene. Begin with a visit to FICO Eataly World, located just outside the city center. This massive food park is a celebration of Italian gastronomy, offering visitors the chance to explore a variety of food pavilions, participate in cooking classes, and even observe food production processes. It's an interactive and educational experience that highlights the richness of Italian cuisine. After a morning at FICO, return to the city for lunch. Consider dining at one of Bologna's renowned trattorias or osterias, where you can enjoy traditional dishes made from recipes passed down through generations. Sampling the local mortadella, balsamic vinegar from nearby Modena, and Parmigiano-Reggiano cheese is essential.

In the afternoon, join a guided food tour or cooking class. These experiences often include visits to local markets, bakeries, and pasta shops, providing a hands-on understanding of Bologna's culinary traditions. Learning to make fresh pasta or a classic Bolognese sauce under the guidance of a local chef is not only fun but also a deeply rewarding way to connect with the city's culture. For dinner, seek out a restaurant known for its innovative takes on traditional dishes. Bologna's food scene is constantly evolving, and many chefs are blending old and new techniques to create unique culinary experiences. This evening, savor a contemporary meal that highlights the best of both worlds.

Day Four: Day Trip to Nearby Destinations

Bologna's central location makes it an ideal base for day trips to other fascinating destinations in the Emilia-Romagna region. One popular option is a visit to Modena, renowned for its balsamic vinegar and automotive heritage. Start the day with a tour of a traditional acetaia, where balsamic vinegar is produced. The intricate process and the rich history of this product are captivating, and tastings offer a deep appreciation for this culinary treasure. After exploring Modena's culinary offerings, visit the Enzo Ferrari Museum to dive into the history of one of Italy's most iconic brands. The museum showcases a stunning collection of Ferrari cars and exhibits detailing the life and achievements of Enzo Ferrari. Alternatively, visitors can take a day trip to Parma, famous for its prosciutto and Parmesan cheese.

A guided tour of a cheese factory or prosciutto production facility provides a fascinating look at the craftsmanship involved in producing these world-famous products. For those interested in a more relaxing day, the charming town of Dozza, with its picturesque streets and medieval fortress, offers a peaceful escape. The town is also known for its vibrant murals, adding a modern twist to its historic charm. Return to Bologna in the evening and enjoy a relaxing dinner at a local eatery, reflecting on the day's adventures and the regional diversity experienced.

Day Five: Final Explorations and Farewell

On the last day in Bologna, take the opportunity to visit any remaining sights and enjoy a leisurely pace. Begin with a visit to the Santo Stefano complex, also known as the "Seven Churches." This unique site comprises multiple interconnected churches and courtyards, each with its own historical and architectural significance. It's a serene and reflective space, perfect for a morning visit. Afterward, explore the Giardini Margherita, Bologna's largest public park. The lush greenery and tranquil atmosphere offer a pleasant contrast to the city's urban energy. It's an ideal spot for a picnic or a leisurely walk, providing a moment of relaxation before departure. For lunch, consider a visit to a local enoteca, where you can sample a variety of wines from the Emilia-Romagna region. Pair the wine with small plates of local cheeses and cured meats, enjoying the flavors of the region in a casual, convivial setting.

In the afternoon, visit the Museum of the History of Bologna, located in the Palazzo Pepoli. This museum offers an engaging and interactive overview of the city's history from ancient times to the present day. It's an excellent way to round off the visit, providing a deeper understanding of Bologna's rich cultural heritage. As the day comes to a close, take a final stroll through the city's streets, soaking in the vibrant atmosphere one last time. Enjoy a farewell dinner at a favorite restaurant, savoring the flavors that have made the visit memorable. Reflect on the experiences and memories created over the past five days, appreciating the unique charm and warmth of Bologna.

5.3 Essential Packing List
Preparing for a trip to Bologna involves thoughtful consideration of various factors, including the city's climate, cultural norms, and the diverse activities one might engage in. From exploring historical sites and indulging in culinary delights to attending local festivals and enjoying the vibrant nightlife, packing appropriately ensures a comfortable and enjoyable experience. This guide offers a comprehensive overview of what to include in your luggage to make the most of your visit to Bologna.

Clothing
Bologna experiences a range of weather conditions throughout the year, necessitating versatile clothing choices. In spring and autumn, the weather is mild, making lightweight layers ideal. Packing a mix of t-shirts, long-sleeve shirts, and light sweaters or jackets allows for easy adaptation to varying

temperatures. Summer can be quite warm, so breathable fabrics like cotton and linen are recommended. Comfortable shorts, skirts, and dresses, along with sun protection such as hats and sunglasses, are essential. Winter in Bologna can be chilly, requiring warmer clothing. Including a good-quality coat, scarves, gloves, and layers like sweaters and thermal wear will keep you comfortable during your explorations.

Footwear

Given Bologna's extensive porticos and cobblestone streets, comfortable walking shoes are a must. Sneakers or well-cushioned walking shoes are ideal for daytime activities, ensuring that your feet are well-supported as you navigate the city. For evening outings or dining at upscale restaurants, consider packing a pair of stylish yet comfortable dress shoes. If you plan on visiting religious sites or partaking in more formal events, conservative footwear is appropriate.

Essential Accessories

Accessories can significantly enhance your travel experience. A reliable daypack or tote bag is useful for carrying daily essentials such as a water bottle, snacks, maps, and travel guides. An umbrella or a compact rain jacket is advisable, particularly during the wetter months. Sunglasses and a hat are crucial for sun protection, especially in the summer. For those planning to document their journey, a good-quality camera with extra memory cards and batteries is essential.

Travel Documents and Money Essentials

Ensuring you have all necessary travel documents is paramount. A valid passport, along with copies of your identification and travel itinerary, should be kept secure. Travel insurance documents and any necessary visas are also crucial. It's wise to carry a combination of payment methods, including credit cards, a debit card, and some local currency for small purchases. A secure travel wallet or money belt can help keep these items safe.

Health and Personal Care Items

Maintaining personal care while traveling requires packing the right health and hygiene products. A basic first aid kit, including band-aids, pain relievers, and any prescription medications, is essential. Personal hygiene products such as toothpaste, toothbrush, deodorant, and shampoo should be included. Sunscreen is important for protecting your skin during outdoor activities. If you have specific skincare or beauty products you prefer, bring them along as familiar brands may not be available locally.

Technology and Communication Tools

Staying connected during your trip necessitates certain technological tools. A smartphone with an international roaming plan or a local SIM card ensures you can make calls, use maps, and access travel apps. Chargers and power adapters compatible with European outlets are essential. A portable power bank can be very handy for long days out. If you plan to work or stay connected online frequently, a lightweight laptop or tablet might be useful.

Cultural and Practical Considerations

Understanding and respecting local customs can enhance your travel experience in Bologna. Modest clothing is advisable when visiting religious sites, with shoulders and knees covered. A scarf or shawl can be useful for this purpose. Learning a few basic Italian phrases can facilitate smoother interactions and is often appreciated by locals. Additionally, familiarizing yourself with local customs regarding dining, tipping, and social etiquette can prevent any unintentional faux pas..

5.4 Visa Requirements and Entry Procedures

Traveling to Bologna, a historic and vibrant city in northern Italy, requires understanding the visa requirements which depend significantly on the traveler's nationality. Citizens of the European Union (EU), European Economic Area (EEA), and Switzerland do not need a visa to enter Italy, including Bologna, for any duration. These travelers can enter with just a valid passport or national identity card. For non-EU nationals, the visa requirements vary. Citizens from countries that are part of the Schengen Agreement, such as the United States, Canada, Australia, and many others, can enter Italy without a visa for tourism or business stays up to 90 days within a 180-day period. However, their passports must be valid for at least three months beyond the planned departure date from the Schengen area.

Travelers from countries that do not have a visa waiver agreement with the Schengen area will need to apply for a Schengen visa prior to arrival. This process involves completing a visa application form, providing a valid passport, two recent passport-sized photos, proof of accommodation in Bologna, a travel itinerary, proof of sufficient financial means, and travel insurance covering medical emergencies. The application should be submitted to the Italian consulate or embassy in the applicant's home country. Processing times can vary, so it's advisable to apply well in advance of the intended travel date.

Entry Procedures to Bologna by Air Travel

Arriving in Bologna by air is a common and convenient option, with Bologna Guglielmo Marconi Airport serving as the main gateway. Upon arrival, passengers will proceed to passport control. EU, EEA, and Swiss nationals can use the EU/EEA lanes, often expedited, while all other travelers must go through the standard immigration checks. At passport control, travelers must present their passports and any required visas. Immigration officers may ask questions about the purpose of the visit, length of stay, and accommodation arrangements. It's essential to have all relevant documents easily accessible. Once cleared through passport control, passengers can proceed to baggage claim to retrieve their luggage.

After collecting luggage, visitors will pass through customs. Italy follows the European Union customs regulations, so travelers need to declare any goods that exceed duty-free allowances. Green channels are for those with nothing to declare, while red channels are for those carrying goods that need to be declared. Customs officers may conduct random checks, so it's important to know the regulations beforehand to avoid any issues.

Entry Procedures to Bologna by Train

Traveling to Bologna by train offers a scenic and comfortable journey, especially from other European countries. Bologna's central train station, Bologna Centrale, is a major hub in Italy's railway network, making it accessible from various international and domestic locations. For those traveling from within the Schengen area, there are generally no border controls, making the process straightforward and hassle-free. Passengers can simply disembark from the train and proceed to their next destination. However, it is recommended to keep identification documents such as a passport or national ID card handy, as random checks can occur. For travelers arriving from non-Schengen countries, passport and visa checks will typically be conducted at the first point of entry into the Schengen area. Once these formalities are completed, subsequent travel to Bologna by train will not involve additional checks. Upon arriving at Bologna Centrale, visitors can find numerous services and facilities, including tourist information centers, to assist with onward travel and local information.

Entry Procedures to Bologna by Road

Entering Bologna by road, whether driving a personal vehicle or taking a bus, provides a different perspective of Italy's landscapes and culture. For those driving from another Schengen country, there are no routine border checks, allowing for a seamless journey into Italy. However, it is essential to carry a valid passport or ID card, as well as a driver's license, vehicle registration documents, and proof of insurance. For travelers coming from non-Schengen countries, border controls will be encountered at the first Schengen entry point. Here, passports and visas will be checked, and customs regulations will apply. Once these procedures are completed, the journey to Bologna can continue without further interruptions. Bus travel into Bologna from neighboring countries follows a similar process. International bus services often stop at the main bus terminals where passport and visa checks occur, particularly when entering from non-Schengen areas. Upon arrival at Bologna's main bus station, travelers will find a range of services, including ticket offices, restrooms, and information desks.

5.5 Safety Tips and Emergency Contacts

aveling to a new city is always an exciting adventure, but ensuring your safety and knowing how to respond in an emergency is crucial for a worry-free trip. Bologna, with its rich history and vibrant atmosphere, is generally a safe destination for travelers. However, being prepared and informed about safety tips and emergency contacts can enhance your experience and provide peace of mind. This guide covers essential safety tips and provides detailed information on emergency contacts to ensure you have a secure and enjoyable visit to Bologna.

General Safety Tips for Exploring Bologna

Bologna, like any major city, requires a combination of common sense and specific precautions to ensure a safe visit. One of the primary considerations for travelers is being aware of their surroundings. Bologna's historic center is bustling with activity, making it a prime spot for pickpockets, especially in crowded areas such as Piazza Maggiore, the markets, and public transportation hubs. Keeping your personal belongings secure and being vigilant can prevent most petty thefts. It's advisable to use a money belt or a secure bag with zippers, and to avoid displaying valuables like expensive jewelry or large amounts of cash.

Emergency Contacts

In case of emergencies, having quick access to important contacts can make a significant difference. Italy has a well-organized emergency response system, and knowing the appropriate numbers to call is crucial. For medical emergencies, dialing 112 connects you to the European emergency number, which can dispatch medical, fire, or police services as needed. Alternatively, dialing 118 will directly connect you to emergency medical services. Bologna's hospitals are well-equipped to handle various medical situations, and some of the prominent ones include Policlinico Sant'Orsola-Malpighi and Ospedale Maggiore. It's reassuring to know that these facilities provide excellent care and many staff members speak English. If you need police assistance, dialing 113 will connect you to the police emergency line. The Carabinieri, another branch of Italy's law enforcement, can be reached at 112. For fire emergencies, you should dial 115. These numbers ensure that help is quickly available, no matter the nature of the emergency.

Health and Medical Precautions

Staying healthy while traveling involves a mix of proactive measures and knowing where to seek help if needed. Before your trip, consider obtaining travel insurance that covers medical expenses and emergencies. This ensures you have access to quality healthcare without worrying about costs. Bologna's pharmacies, marked by a green cross, are widely available and can provide over-the-counter medications for minor ailments. Pharmacists in Italy are well-trained and can offer advice on common health issues. If you require prescription medication, bring enough to last your trip, along with a copy of the prescription. In the event of a serious medical issue, head to one of Bologna's major hospitals. Familiarize yourself with the location of these hospitals and keep their contact information handy. Additionally, knowing basic Italian phrases related to health can be helpful, though many medical professionals speak English.

5.6 Currency Exchange and Banking Services
Understanding the local currency, banking options, budgeting tips, and other money-related matters can significantly enhance your travel experience. This comprehensive guide provides detailed information on these aspects, helping you navigate Bologna with financial confidence.

Local Currency
Italy uses the Euro (€) as its official currency, and Bologna is no exception. The Euro is divided into 100 cents, with coins in denominations of 1, 2, 5, 10, 20, and 50 cents, and 1 and 2 Euros. Banknotes come in denominations of 5, 10, 20, 50, 100, 200, and 500 Euros. It's advisable to familiarize yourself with the appearance and value of these notes and coins to avoid confusion during transactions.

When arriving in Bologna, having some Euros in cash can be helpful for small purchases, tips, and transportation fares. Currency exchange services are available at the airport, train stations, and various locations throughout the city. However, for better rates, it might be beneficial to use ATMs or withdraw cash from your home country before traveling.

Banking Services for Travelers
Bologna is home to several major banks that cater to both locals and visitors, offering a range of services from currency exchange to international banking.

Here are five prominent banks in Bologna that provide special services for travelers:

UniCredit; is one of the largest banks in Italy and offers comprehensive banking services, including currency exchange and ATM withdrawals. Their branches are conveniently located throughout Bologna, with a major branch at Via Ugo Bassi, 1. UniCredit also provides multi-language ATMs and customer service, making it accessible for international visitors.

Intesa Sanpaolo; is another major bank that provides extensive services for travelers. With branches like the one at Via Rizzoli, 8, Intesa Sanpaolo offers currency exchange, international money transfers, and ATMs that accept major international cards. Their banking app also supports multiple languages, facilitating easier transactions for non-Italian speakers.

BPER Banca; is known for its excellent customer service and comprehensive banking solutions. Located at Via Indipendenza, 11, BPER Banca provides currency exchange, international wire transfers, and ATMs with instructions in several languages. They also offer travel insurance and other services tailored to travelers' needs.

BNL (Banca Nazionale del Lavoro); part of the BNP Paribas group, has a strong presence in Bologna with services that include currency exchange, ATMs, and international banking assistance. Their branch at Via Luigi Carlo Farini, 1, is centrally located and easily accessible for tourists.

Banco BPM; offers a range of banking services, including currency exchange and multi-currency accounts. Their branch at Via Irnerio, 20, provides convenient access to banking services for international visitors, with staff who can assist in multiple languages.

These banks, along with their widespread ATMs, make accessing your funds straightforward and secure while in Bologna. It's advisable to notify your home bank of your travel plans to avoid any disruptions in service.

Budgeting for Your Bologna Adventure
Creating a budget for your trip to Bologna can help manage expenses and ensure a worry-free experience. Bologna is known for its affordability compared to other major Italian cities, but costs can vary depending on your preferences and activities. Accommodation can range from budget-friendly hostels and mid-range hotels to luxury stays. It's wise to book in advance to secure the best rates. Meals in Bologna are a highlight, with options ranging from inexpensive trattorias and pizzerias to high-end dining. Street food and local markets offer delicious and affordable options for those looking to save.

Transportation costs are relatively low, with efficient public transport and walkable distances between major attractions. Purchasing a Bologna Welcome Card can provide discounts on public transportation and entry to various museums and landmarks, offering additional savings. When it comes to shopping, Bologna offers everything from high-end boutiques to local markets. Budgeting for souvenirs and personal shopping is essential, as it's easy to get tempted by the city's vibrant retail scene.

Bureau de Change Locations in Bologna
For travelers who prefer to exchange currency upon arrival, Bologna has several Bureau de Change locations that offer competitive rates and convenient services. These can be found at major transportation hubs like Bologna Centrale train station and Bologna Guglielmo Marconi Airport. Additionally, there are several reputable exchange offices throughout the city center, such as Forexchange at Via Ugo Bassi, 10, and Best and Fast Change at Piazza Maggiore, 1. These locations typically offer extended hours and multilingual staff to assist travelers.

Managing Money and Avoiding Fees

To minimize transaction fees, consider using a travel-friendly bank account or credit card that offers low or no foreign transaction fees. Many banks provide special travel cards that can be preloaded with Euros, allowing you to manage your budget more effectively and avoid fluctuating exchange rates. When withdrawing cash, use bank-affiliated ATMs rather than standalone machines to avoid higher fees and ensure better security. It's also prudent to carry a mix of payment methods, including cash, credit, and debit cards, to be prepared for different scenarios.

5.7 Language, Communication and Useful Phrases

Bologna offers a unique blend of historical charm and modern dynamism. For visitors, understanding the local language and communication nuances can significantly enhance the experience, enabling deeper connections with the city and its people.

Language and Communication in Bologna

Italian is the official language of Bologna, and while English is spoken in many tourist areas, especially among younger generations and in the hospitality industry, having some basic knowledge of Italian can be incredibly beneficial. The Bolognese are known for their warm and welcoming nature, and making an effort to speak their language is often appreciated and can open doors to more authentic interactions.

Essential Italian Phrases

When visiting Bologna, certain phrases can be particularly useful. Greeting someone with a friendly "Buongiorno" (Good morning) or "Buonasera" (Good evening) sets a positive tone. "Per favore" (Please) and "Grazie" (Thank you) are essential for polite exchanges. Inquiring about directions with "Dove si trova...?" (Where is...?) or asking for assistance with "Può aiutarmi?" (Can you help me?) can be very helpful. When dining, phrases like "Vorrei ordinare..." (I would like to order...) and "Il conto, per favore" (The check, please) are practical.

Cultural Etiquette

Understanding local customs and etiquette is crucial for a respectful and enjoyable visit. In Bologna, as in the rest of Italy, greetings often involve a handshake, and among friends or closer acquaintances, cheek kisses are common. It is customary to address people with their titles, such as "Signore" (Mr.) or "Signora" (Mrs.), unless invited to use first names.

Practical Tips for Visitors

Staying connected in Bologna is facilitated by widespread availability of Wi-Fi, particularly in hotels, cafes, and public spaces. Currency exchange and ATM services are readily accessible, and credit cards are widely accepted. Learning a few Italian phrases related to money transactions, like "Quanto costa?" (How much does it cost?) and "Posso pagare con carta di credito?" (Can I pay with a credit card?), can ease financial interactions.

5.8 Shopping and Souvenirs

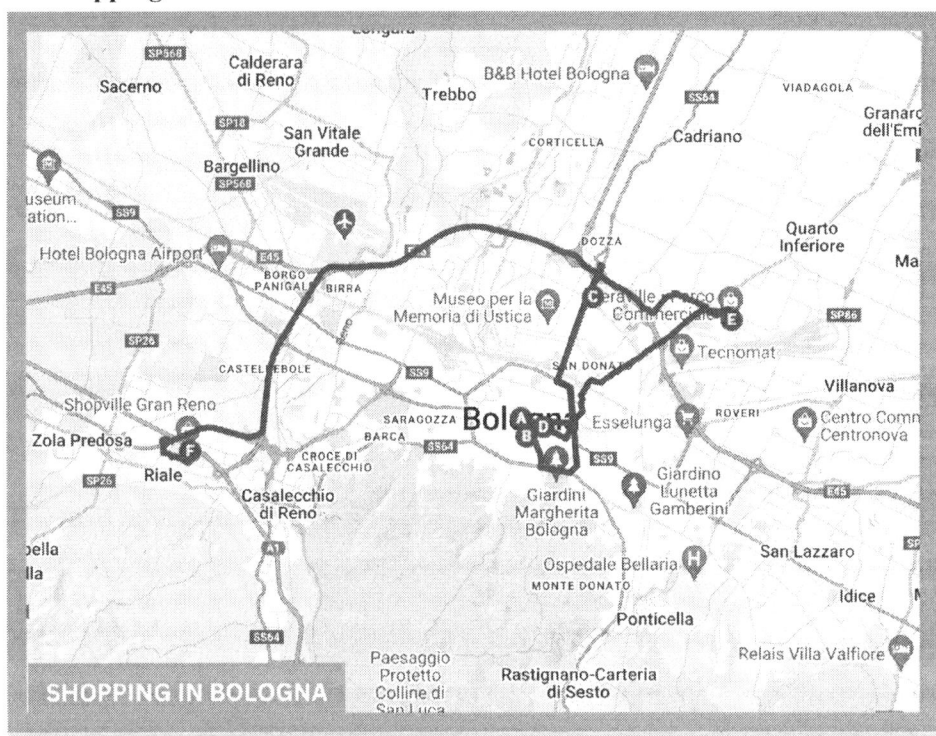

Directions from Bologna, Metropolitan City of Bologna, Italy to Shopvile Gran Reno, Via Marilyn Monroe, Casalecchio di Reno, Metropolitan City of Bologna, Italy

A
Bologna, Metropolitan City of Bologna, Italy

B
Galleria Cavour, Via Farini, Bologna, Metropolitan City of Bologna, Italy

C
Parco Commerciale Borgo Mascarella, Via Stalingrado, Bologna, Metropolitan City of Bologna, Italy

D
Corte Isolani, Bologna, Metropolitan City of Bologna, Italy

E
Meraville Parco Commerciale, Viale Tito Carnacini, Bologna, Metropolitan City of Bologna, Italy

F
Shopville Gran Reno, Via Marilyn Monroe, Casalecchio di Reno, Metropolitan City of Bologna, Italy

Exploring the shopping districts of Bologna provides a unique opportunity to discover local craftsmanship, culinary delights, and fashionable finds. This guide highlights distinct shopping destinations in Bologna, each offering a unique selection of goods and products.

Galleria Cavour

Located in the heart of Bologna's historic center, Galleria Cavour is a prestigious shopping arcade renowned for its high-end boutiques and luxury brands. Situated near Piazza Maggiore, this elegant gallery features designer stores offering clothing, accessories, and jewelry from renowned Italian and international brands. Visitors can explore upscale fashion labels such as Gucci, Prada, and Louis Vuitton, alongside exclusive Italian designers. Prices here tend to be higher, reflecting the premium quality and craftsmanship of the products. Galleria Cavour typically opens from 10 AM to 8 PM, Monday to Saturday. Travelers can easily access this shopping destination by foot from major landmarks in the city center.

Parco Commerciale Borgo

For those seeking a more comprehensive shopping experience, Parco Commerciale Borgo offers a vast selection of retail outlets and dining options. Located on the outskirts of Bologna, this modern shopping complex features a mix of international chains and Italian brands, making it a popular destination for locals and tourists alike. Visitors can browse a wide range of goods, including clothing, electronics, home furnishings, and beauty products, all conveniently located under one roof. Prices at Parco Commerciale Borgo vary depending on the stores and products, with options available for different budgets. The complex typically operates from 9 AM to 9 PM, seven days a week, providing ample flexibility for shopping excursions. Travelers can reach Parco Commerciale Borgo by car or public transportation, with ample parking available on-site.

Corte Isolani

Corte Isolani offers a charming blend of boutique shops and artisanal stores. This picturesque courtyard, surrounded by medieval buildings, is a hidden gem for shoppers seeking unique souvenirs and locally crafted goods. Visitors can explore quaint shops selling handmade jewelry, leather goods, ceramics, and gourmet food products, all crafted by local artisans. Prices at Corte Isolani vary depending on the craftsmanship and materials used, with options available for every budget. The shops here typically open from 10 AM to 7 PM, Tuesday to Sunday. Travelers can easily access Corte Isolani on foot from Piazza Maggiore, immersing themselves in the historic ambiance of Bologna's oldest market district.

Meraville Parco Commerciale

Situated on the outskirts of Bologna, Meraville Parco Commerciale is a sprawling shopping complex offering a diverse range of retail options. From fashion outlets and home decor stores to electronics shops and specialty boutiques, Meraville caters to a wide range of shopping preferences. Visitors can enjoy discounted prices on popular brands and take advantage of the numerous dining and entertainment options available within the complex. Meraville Parco Commerciale operates from 9 AM to 9 PM, seven days a week, providing ample time for shopping and leisure activities. Travelers can access Meraville Parco Commerciale by car or public transportation, with convenient parking facilities available on-site.

Shopville Gran Reno

Located just outside the city center, Shopville Gran Reno is one of Bologna's largest shopping centers, offering a comprehensive retail experience for visitors. With over 130 stores, including fashion boutiques, electronics outlets, and specialty shops, Shopville Gran Reno caters to diverse shopping needs. Visitors can find a wide range of products at competitive prices, from clothing and accessories to home furnishings and sporting goods. The center also features a food court and entertainment facilities, making it a popular destination for families and leisure shoppers. Shopville Gran Reno typically opens from 9 AM to 9 PM, Monday to Saturday. Travelers can easily access the shopping center by car or public transportation, with ample parking available on-site.

5.9 Health and Wellness Centers
Bologna also offers an impressive array of health and wellness centers catering to the needs of visitors seeking relaxation, rejuvenation, and holistic well-being. From luxurious spas to holistic wellness retreats, the city provides a diverse range of options for those looking to enhance their physical and mental health during their stay.

Terme San Petronio
Located in the heart of Bologna, Terme San Petronio offers a sanctuary of relaxation and therapeutic treatments. This wellness center is famed for its thermal baths, which utilize mineral-rich waters known for their healing properties. Visitors can indulge in various hydrotherapy treatments, including thermal baths, steam rooms, and saunas, which promote relaxation and detoxification. The center also offers a range of massages, from traditional Swedish to deep tissue, each designed to alleviate stress and tension. The tranquil ambiance, combined with expert care from trained therapists, ensures a deeply restorative experience.

Beyond hydrotherapy, Terme San Petronio provides beauty treatments such as facials and body scrubs, incorporating natural ingredients to nourish and rejuvenate the skin. The holistic approach extends to their wellness programs, which include yoga and meditation sessions aimed at promoting mental clarity and balance. This combination of physical and mental wellness services makes Terme San Petronio a comprehensive health haven for visitors.

Villaggio della Salute Più

Villaggio della Salute Più is an expansive wellness retreat offering a holistic approach to health. The center features thermal pools fed by natural hot springs, known for their therapeutic benefits. Guests can immerse themselves in these healing waters, enjoying the serene natural surroundings that enhance the sense of tranquility and rejuvenation. Villaggio della Salute Più goes beyond thermal treatments, offering a variety of wellness programs tailored to individual needs. These programs include nutritional counseling, fitness training, and stress management workshops. The center's philosophy emphasizes the importance of a balanced lifestyle, combining physical activities such as hiking and cycling with relaxation therapies like massages and aromatherapy.

MySelf Wellness Center

MySelf Wellness Center, situated in the city center, offers a modern and holistic approach to health and wellness. This contemporary facility is equipped with state-of-the-art fitness equipment and provides a range of classes, including yoga, Pilates, and high-intensity interval training (HIIT). The center's team of professional trainers and therapists work closely with visitors to create personalized fitness and wellness plans tailored to their specific goals. In addition to fitness training, MySelf Wellness Center offers a variety of therapeutic services designed to promote overall well-being. These include physiotherapy, chiropractic care, and osteopathy, which are particularly beneficial for those recovering from injuries or experiencing chronic pain. The center also provides nutritional counseling to help visitors adopt healthier eating habits that support their fitness and wellness objectives.

Oasi Spa at the Grand Hotel Majestic

Located within the luxurious Grand Hotel Majestic, the Oasi Spa offers a high-end wellness experience characterized by elegance and sophistication. The spa's serene and opulent environment provides the perfect setting for a range of exclusive treatments designed to pamper and rejuvenate. Guests can choose from a variety of massages, facials, and body treatments, all using premium products to ensure the highest quality care. One of the standout features of Oasi Spa is its personalized approach to wellness. The spa's experienced therapists conduct thorough consultations to understand each guest's needs and preferences, tailoring treatments to provide maximum benefit. In addition to traditional spa services, Oasi Spa offers specialized treatments such as anti-aging therapies, detox programs, and holistic healing sessions.

Ayurvedic Center Bologna

For visitors interested in holistic and alternative medicine, the Ayurvedic Center Bologna provides an authentic and comprehensive approach to health and wellness based on ancient Indian traditions. This center specializes in Ayurvedic treatments, which focus on balancing the body's energies to promote overall health and prevent disease. Visitors can experience a range of therapies, including Abhyanga (Ayurvedic massage), Shirodhara (forehead oil pouring), and Panchakarma (detoxification programs). The Ayurvedic Center Bologna emphasizes personalized care, with consultations conducted by experienced practitioners who assess each individual's unique constitution and health needs. Based on this assessment, a tailored treatment plan is created, incorporating diet, lifestyle recommendations, and specific Ayurvedic therapies to restore balance and harmony.

5.10 Useful Websites, Mobile Apps and Online Resources

Planning a trip to Bologna involves more than just booking flights and accommodations. With the plethora of information available online, leveraging useful websites, mobile apps, and online resources can greatly enhance your travel experience. From finding the best restaurants to navigating public transportation, these digital tools provide valuable assistance to ensure you make the most of your time in Bologna.

Official Tourism Websites

The official tourism website of Bologna, managed by Bologna Welcome, is an indispensable resource for travelers. Here, you can find comprehensive information on attractions, events, accommodations, dining options, and more. The website offers interactive maps, suggested itineraries, and practical tips for exploring the city. Additionally, Bologna Welcome provides assistance in multiple languages, making it accessible to international visitors. Bookmarking this website before your trip will serve as a valuable reference throughout your stay in Bologna.

Interactive Maps and Navigation Apps

Navigating the streets of Bologna can be made easier with interactive maps and navigation apps. Google Maps is a popular choice, offering detailed maps, real-time traffic updates, and directions for walking, driving, and public transportation. With offline capabilities, you can download maps of Bologna in advance and access them without an internet connection. Another option is Citymapper, which provides comprehensive public transportation information, including schedules, routes, and fare estimates. These apps are invaluable for getting around the city efficiently and discovering its hidden gems.

Dining and Restaurant Reservation Apps

Exploring Bologna's culinary scene is a must-do for any visitor. To find the best restaurants and make reservations effortlessly, consider using dining and restaurant reservation apps. TripAdvisor and Yelp are reliable platforms for reading reviews, browsing photos, and finding restaurants that suit your preferences and budget. Additionally, apps like TheFork allow you to book tables at popular eateries with ease, often offering exclusive discounts and deals for users. Whether you're craving traditional Italian cuisine or international fare, these apps help you plan memorable dining experiences in Bologna.

Local Events and Activities Apps

To stay updated on events, festivals, and activities happening in Bologna during your visit, turn to local events and activities apps. Eventbrite and Meetup are excellent platforms for discovering a diverse range of events, from cultural exhibitions to live music performances and outdoor markets. You can filter events by date, location, and category, ensuring you don't miss out on any exciting happenings in Bologna. Additionally, Bologna's official tourism website often features a calendar of events, providing valuable insights into the city's cultural calendar.

Language Translation and Communication Apps

While English is widely spoken in tourist areas of Bologna, having a language translation and communication app can be helpful for overcoming language barriers and communicating with locals. Apps like Google Translate offer instant translation for text, speech, and images, allowing you to easily communicate in Italian or other languages. Duolingo is another useful app for learning basic Italian phrases and improving your language skills before and during your trip. With these apps at your fingertips, you can engage with locals, navigate menus, and ask for directions with confidence.

5.11 Internet Access and Connectivity

Ensuring reliable internet access and connectivity is essential for visitors to Bologna, whether they are traveling for business or leisure. Fortunately, the city offers a variety of options to stay connected, ranging from Wi-Fi hotspots to mobile data plans and internet cafes.

Wi-Fi Hotspots

Bologna boasts a widespread network of Wi-Fi hotspots, providing convenient internet access in public spaces, hotels, restaurants, and cafes throughout the city. Many hotels offer complimentary Wi-Fi access to guests, allowing visitors to stay connected from the comfort of their accommodations. Additionally, major tourist attractions, such as Piazza Maggiore and the Two Towers, often provide free Wi-Fi access to visitors, enabling them to share their experiences in real-time and stay connected with friends and family back home.

Mobile Data Plans

For visitors who require constant internet access on the go, purchasing a local SIM card and data plan is a convenient option. Several mobile operators in Italy offer prepaid SIM cards with data packages that provide reliable internet connectivity throughout Bologna and the surrounding areas. These SIM cards can be easily purchased at convenience stores, tobacco shops, or mobile network stores, and typically require a valid passport for registration. With a local SIM card and data plan, visitors can enjoy seamless internet access for navigation, communication, and browsing during their stay in Bologna.

Internet Cafes

Although internet cafes are becoming less common with the widespread availability of Wi-Fi and mobile data, Bologna still has a few establishments where visitors can access the internet for a nominal fee. These cafes typically offer computer terminals with internet access, allowing travelers to check emails, surf the web, or print documents if needed. Internet cafes are particularly useful for visitors who do not have their own devices or require access to specialized software or services during their stay.

Co-working Spaces

For digital nomads, freelancers, or business travelers in need of a dedicated workspace with reliable internet access, Bologna offers several co-working spaces equipped with high-speed Wi-Fi, comfortable workstations, and amenities such as meeting rooms, printing facilities, and refreshments. These spaces provide a productive environment for remote work or collaborative projects, allowing visitors to maintain their productivity while exploring the city. Some co-working spaces also host networking events, workshops, and community gatherings, providing opportunities to connect with like-minded individuals and professionals.

Public Libraries

Bologna's public libraries offer another option for visitors seeking internet access and connectivity. The Biblioteca Sala Borsa, located in the historic city center, is one of the city's main libraries and provides free Wi-Fi access to patrons. Visitors can bring their own devices or use library computers to access the internet, research local attractions, or catch up on work or studies. The library's quiet and tranquil atmosphere makes it an ideal place to work or study while enjoying access to a reliable internet connection.

5.12 Visitor Centers and Tourist Assistance

Bologna is home to several well-established visitor centers strategically located to provide maximum convenience for tourists. These centers are equipped with multilingual staff who are knowledgeable about the city's offerings and are eager to assist visitors in making the most of their stay.

Bologna Welcome Center

One prominent visitor center is the Bologna Welcome Center located at Piazza Maggiore 1/e. Situated in the heart of the city, this center is ideally positioned for tourists arriving in the central historic area. The staff here provide comprehensive information on city tours, cultural events, and local attractions. Additionally, they offer ticketing services for museums and public transportation, making it a one-stop-shop for all tourist needs.

Bologna Centrale Train Station

Another significant center is found at the Bologna Centrale Train Station, Piazza delle Medaglie d'Oro 4. This center caters to the needs of visitors arriving by train, offering information on transportation options, accommodations, and city tours. The strategic location ensures that travelers can quickly access assistance as soon as they arrive in the city.

Bologna Welcome Point

The Bologna Welcome Point at Guglielmo Marconi Airport is another crucial resource for tourists. Located in the arrivals area, this center provides first-time visitors with essential information and maps, helping them navigate the city from the moment they land. The staff can assist with transportation arrangements and offer guidance on the best ways to reach the city center and other key destinations.

Tourist Information Office

For visitors exploring the outskirts of Bologna, the Tourist Information Office at Piazza Maggiore 6 is particularly useful. This center focuses on providing information about the surrounding region, including the Emilia-Romagna countryside and nearby towns. The staff can suggest day trips and excursions, enhancing the overall travel experience by introducing visitors to the broader cultural landscape.

Bologna Fiere

Lastly, the Bologna Fiere Tourist Information Point at Viale della Fiera 20 is essential for those attending events and exhibitions. Located within the city's major exhibition center, this point offers specific assistance related to the various fairs and events hosted in Bologna, providing logistical support and event-specific information.

Special Services of Tourist Assistants

Tourist assistants in Bologna provide a range of specialized services designed to cater to diverse visitor needs. These services extend beyond basic information provision to include personalized travel planning, cultural interpretation, and emergency assistance. The multilingual staff, proficient in English, French, German, and other languages, ensure that language barriers do not hinder the visitor experience. One of the key services offered is personalized itinerary planning.

Tourist assistants can help visitors design custom itineraries that align with their interests, whether it's historical tours, culinary adventures, or art and music experiences. This service is particularly beneficial for first-time visitors who may feel overwhelmed by the array of options available in Bologna. Cultural interpretation is another vital service provided by tourist assistants. Understanding the local customs and cultural nuances can significantly enhance the visitor experience. Tourist assistants offer insights into Bolognese traditions, etiquette, and social norms, enabling visitors to engage more deeply with the local culture.

CHAPTER 6
CULINARY DELIGHTS

6.1 Traditional Bolognese Cuisine

Bolognese cuisine stands out as a true embodiment of Italian gastronomy. As visitors wander through the cobblestone streets and picturesque piazzas, they are greeted by the tantalizing aromas wafting from the city's trattorias and osterias, where centuries-old recipes are lovingly preserved and passed down through generations.

Tagliatelle al Ragu

One cannot embark on a culinary journey through Bologna without indulging in Tagliatelle al Ragu, the quintessential dish of the region. Sold in quaint family-run trattorias and upscale restaurants alike, this iconic pasta dish features freshly made tagliatelle noodles smothered in a hearty meat-based ragu sauce. The ragu, simmered for hours to perfection, boasts a symphony of flavors derived from tender cuts of beef, pork, and veal, harmoniously melded with tomatoes, onions, carrots, and aromatic herbs. Prices for this delectable dish vary depending on the establishment, ranging from €10 to €20 per serving.

Tortellini en Brodo

Another beloved staple of Bolognese cuisine is Tortellini en Brodo, a comforting dish that warms the soul, particularly during the winter months. This simple yet elegant creation features delicate parcels of handmade pasta filled with a savory mixture of prosciutto, Parmigiano-Reggiano cheese, and nutmeg, gently floating in a fragrant, golden-hued broth. Sold in traditional trattorias and local markets across the city, Tortellini en Brodo embodies the essence of Italian home cooking, offering a taste of nostalgia with every spoonful. Prices typically range from €8 to €15 per serving, depending on the venue and accompanying side dishes.

Lasagne alla Bolognese

A symphony of flavors and textures awaits those who partake in Lasagne alla Bolognese, a beloved dish that epitomizes the artistry of Bolognese cuisine. Crafted with layers of fresh pasta sheets, creamy bechamel sauce, and a rich meat ragu, this culinary masterpiece is a feast for both the eyes and the taste buds. Sold in trattorias and osterias throughout Bologna, Lasagne alla Bolognese is often featured as a centerpiece of traditional Sunday lunches and festive gatherings, where families come together to celebrate the joys of food and fellowship. Prices for this indulgent dish typically range from €12 to €25 per serving, depending on the establishment's ambiance and culinary reputation.

Tigelle e Crescentine

For those seeking a taste of Bologna's rustic charm, Tigelle e Crescentine offers a savory journey into the heart of Emilia-Romagna's countryside. These traditional flatbreads, served alongside an array of savory accompaniments such as cured meats, cheeses, and pickled vegetables, embody the region's agrarian heritage and culinary ingenuity. Sold in rustic trattorias and street food stalls known as tigellerias, Tigelle e Crescentine beckon travelers to indulge in a casual yet flavorful dining experience, where simplicity meets satisfaction. Prices for this rustic delight vary depending on the assortment of toppings and condiments, typically ranging from €8 to €15 per serving.

6.2 Local Delicacies: Mortadella, Crescentine

Bologna, affectionately known as "La Grassa" (The Fat), is a culinary paradise where every corner brims with tantalizing aromas and delectable flavors. Among the plethora of culinary delights that adorn the tables of Bologna, five local delicacies stand out: Mortadella, Crescentine, Tortellini, Tagliatelle al Ragu, and Gelato.

Mortadella

One cannot embark on a culinary journey through Bologna without savoring its iconic Mortadella. Renowned worldwide as the ancestor of modern-day bologna sausage, Mortadella is a quintessential Italian cold cut crafted from finely ground pork, seasoned with spices, and studded with delicate cubes of pork fat. The result is a succulent, pink-hued delicacy that melts in the mouth, bursting with savory flavors. For an authentic experience, head to the historic Quadrilatero market, where seasoned artisans proudly display their prized Mortadella wheels. Prices vary depending on quality and quantity, but expect to pay around €20-€30 per kilogram. When indulging in this gastronomic marvel, remember to pair it with a glass of Lambrusco, a sparkling red wine native to the Emilia-Romagna region, for a truly harmonious symphony of flavors.

Crescentine

No culinary journey through Bologna would be complete without sampling Crescentine, a beloved local specialty adored for its simplicity and rustic charm.

These fluffy, fried bread pockets, also known as "gnocco fritto," are a staple accompaniment to Bologna's hearty meals. Made from a dough of flour, yeast, water, and lard, Crescentine are deep-fried to golden perfection, resulting in a crispy exterior that gives way to a soft, pillowy center. While Crescentine can be found in various trattorias and osterias throughout the city, venture off the beaten path to discover hidden gems like Osteria dell'Orsa, where you can enjoy a generous serving alongside a selection of cured meats and cheeses for approximately €5-€8. For the ultimate indulgence, pair Crescentine with a generous dollop of creamy stracchino cheese and a sprinkle of freshly ground black pepper.

Tortellini

Bologna's culinary legacy is incomplete without paying homage to its illustrious Tortellini. These delicate parcels of pasta, traditionally filled with a sumptuous blend of prosciutto, mortadella, and Parmigiano-Reggiano cheese, are a testament to the city's rich gastronomic heritage. While Tortellini can be enjoyed in various forms, from broth-based soups to decadent cream sauces, purists swear by the classic Tortellini en brodo, served in a rich capon broth. For a taste of tradition, visit Al Sangiovese, a cozy trattoria nestled in the heart of Bologna's historic center, where you can savor a steaming bowl of Tortellini en brodo for approximately €10-€15. When dining out, remember to embrace the Italian philosophy of "al dente," ensuring that your Tortellini retains a firm yet tender texture that tantalizes the taste buds with every bite.

Tagliatelle al Ragu

In the realm of Italian cuisine, few dishes rival the timeless elegance of Tagliatelle al Ragu. Hailing from Bologna's culinary repertoire, this heavenly marriage of silky homemade pasta and slow-cooked meat ragu epitomizes comfort food at its finest. The secret to the dish's unparalleled depth of flavor lies in the ragu, a labor of love crafted from a harmonious blend of tender beef, aromatic vegetables, and velvety tomato sauce, simmered to perfection over low heat. While Tagliatelle al Ragu can be found in trattorias and ristorantes across the city, discerning food enthusiasts flock to Trattoria Anna Maria, a revered culinary institution renowned for its authentic renditions of Bolognese classics. Prices typically range from €12-€18 per serving, making it an affordable yet indulgent dining experience that transports the palate to the sun-kissed hills of Emilia-Romagna.

Gelato

No culinary odyssey through Bologna would be complete without a refreshing scoop of Gelato, Italy's iconic frozen treat that captivates the senses with its vibrant colors and luscious flavors. Unlike conventional ice cream, Gelato boasts a lower fat content and a denser, creamier texture, thanks to the absence of excessive air incorporation during the churning process. For a taste of Gelato nirvana, head to Cremeria Santo Stefano, a charming gelateria nestled near the eponymous basilica, where you can delight in a dazzling array of artisanal flavors, from creamy pistachio to tangy lemon sorbet. Prices typically range from €2-€4 per scoop, making Gelato an affordable indulgence that offers a moment of pure bliss amidst the bustling streets of Bologna.

6.3 Enogastronomic Tours and Wine Tastings

Enogastronomic Tours and Wine Tastings offer an unparalleled experience, Each tour encapsulates the essence of Bologna's culinary traditions, weaving together history, culture, and, of course, delectable food and wine.

Wine & Dine in Bologna

The "Wine & Dine in Bologna" Tour stands out as a quintessential introduction to the city's gastronomic wonders. Sold by local tour operators, this tour typically ranges from €80 to €120 per person, depending on the duration and inclusions. Participants are guided through the charming streets of Bologna, where they have the opportunity to savor an array of traditional dishes paired with exquisite local wines. From creamy Parmigiano Reggiano to succulent prosciutto, each bite tells a story of centuries-old culinary craftsmanship. Tips for visitors embarking on this tour include wearing comfortable walking shoes, as the itinerary often includes strolling through cobblestone alleyways and bustling markets.

Wine Trails of the Emilia-Romagna Countryside

For those with a penchant for culinary exploration beyond the city limits, the "Wine Trails of the Emilia-Romagna Countryside" offers a delightful escape into the region's picturesque vineyards and wineries. Sold by specialized tour operators, prices typically range from €150 to €250 per person, inclusive of transportation and tastings. This immersive experience allows participants to witness firsthand the winemaking process, from vine to bottle, while indulging in the finest vintages accompanied by local delicacies. Visitors should keep in mind that these tours may involve moderate physical activity, such as walking through vineyards or climbing stairs in historic cellars, so dressing accordingly is advisable.

Private Wine Tasting & Cooking Class

For a truly bespoke culinary adventure, the "Private Wine Tasting & Cooking Class" offers a personalized journey into the heart of Bolognese cuisine. Available through select tour operators or private chefs, prices for this exclusive experience can vary depending on group size and customization, often starting from €300 per person. Participants are treated to an intimate cooking session led by a local chef, where they learn to prepare signature dishes like handmade pasta and traditional sauces. This hands-on approach provides invaluable insight into the nuances of Italian cooking, complemented by guided tastings of regional wines. Visitors interested in booking this experience should inquire about dietary restrictions in advance to ensure a tailored culinary experience.

Historical Wine Cellars Tour

For wine enthusiasts seeking a deeper understanding of Bologna's viticultural heritage, the "Historical Wine Cellars Tour" offers a fascinating glimpse into the city's winemaking legacy. Available through various tour operators or directly from historic wineries, prices typically range from €50 to €80 per person, inclusive of guided tours and tastings. Participants are led through ancient cellars dating back centuries, where they discover the secrets behind Bologna's most prized varietals. From robust Sangiovese to delicate Pignoletto, each wine tells a story of terroir and tradition. Visitors should note that some cellars may have limited accessibility, so contacting the operator in advance is recommended, especially for individuals with mobility concerns.

Gourmet Food & Wine Walking Tour

Lastly, for a sensory journey through the flavors of Emilia-Romagna, the "Gourmet Food & Wine Walking Tour" offers an immersive experience blending culinary delights with cultural insights. Sold by local tour companies, prices typically range from €60 to €100 per person, inclusive of tastings and guided tours. Participants meander through Bologna's historic center, stopping at renowned eateries and enotecas to sample an array of regional specialties, from tangy balsamic vinegar to velvety gelato. Tips for visitors embarking on this tour include arriving with an empty stomach and an open mind, ready to savor every moment of this gastronomic adventure.

6.4 Gelato and Pasticcerie: Sweet Treats in Bologna

Bologna extends its gastronomic delights beyond savory dishes to encompass an array of sweet treats that captivate the senses. From velvety gelato to delicate pastries, Bologna's gelaterias and pasticcerie beckon visitors on a journey of indulgence and delight. As travelers meander through the city's charming streets and vibrant piazzas, they are met with an irresistible array of confections that reflect the city's rich culinary heritage and artisanal craftsmanship.

Gelateria Gianni

Gelateria Gianni stands as a testament to the artistry of gelato-making. With a dedication to using only the finest locally sourced ingredients and time-honored techniques, Gelateria Gianni has garnered acclaim for its unparalleled flavors and creamy textures. Visitors can savor a myriad of gelato flavors, from classic favorites like pistachio and stracciatella to innovative creations such as ricotta and fig. Prices at Gelateria Gianni typically range from €2.50 to €4 for a small cone or cup, offering affordable indulgence for discerning palates.

To fully appreciate the experience at Gelateria Gianni, visitors are advised to arrive early, as the gelateria tends to attract a loyal following of locals and tourists alike, especially during peak hours. Additionally, take advantage of the opportunity to sample multiple flavors before making a decision, allowing for a truly customized and satisfying gelato experience.

Pasticceria Gamberini

For aficionados of artisanal pastries and baked goods, Pasticceria Gamberini stands as a beacon of tradition and quality in Bologna. Established in 1907, this iconic pasticceria has been delighting patrons with its exquisite selection of cakes, pastries, and cookies for over a century. From delicate mille-feuille to decadent chocolate eclairs, each creation at Pasticceria Gamberini reflects a commitment to time-honored recipes and superior craftsmanship. Prices for pastries and cakes vary depending on size and complexity, typically ranging from €2 to €5 per item.

Cremeria Funivia

For those seeking a truly elevated gelato experience, Cremeria Funivia offers a tantalizing array of artisanal flavors crafted with precision and passion. Located near Bologna's iconic San Luca Basilica, this gelateria combines traditional techniques with modern innovation to create gelato masterpieces that delight the senses. From creamy classics like stracciatella and hazelnut to adventurous flavors like saffron and rosemary, Cremeria Funivia offers something for every palate. Prices at Cremeria Funivia typically range from €3 to €5 for a small cone or cup, reflecting the premium quality and craftsmanship of their gelato.

Pasticceria Santo Stefano

Tucked away in the charming Santo Stefano neighborhood, Pasticceria Santo Stefano invites visitors to indulge in a delectable assortment of pastries, cakes, and cookies in a quaint and cozy setting. With a focus on using locally sourced ingredients and traditional recipes passed down through generations, this beloved pasticceria captures the essence of Bologna's culinary heritage with each delightful creation. From flaky sfogliatelle to buttery brioche, Pasticceria Santo Stefano offers a taste of nostalgia with every bite. Prices for pastries and cakes typically range from €1.50 to €4 per item, making it an affordable luxury for visitors.

6.5 Michelin-Starred Restaurants and Gastronomic Experiences

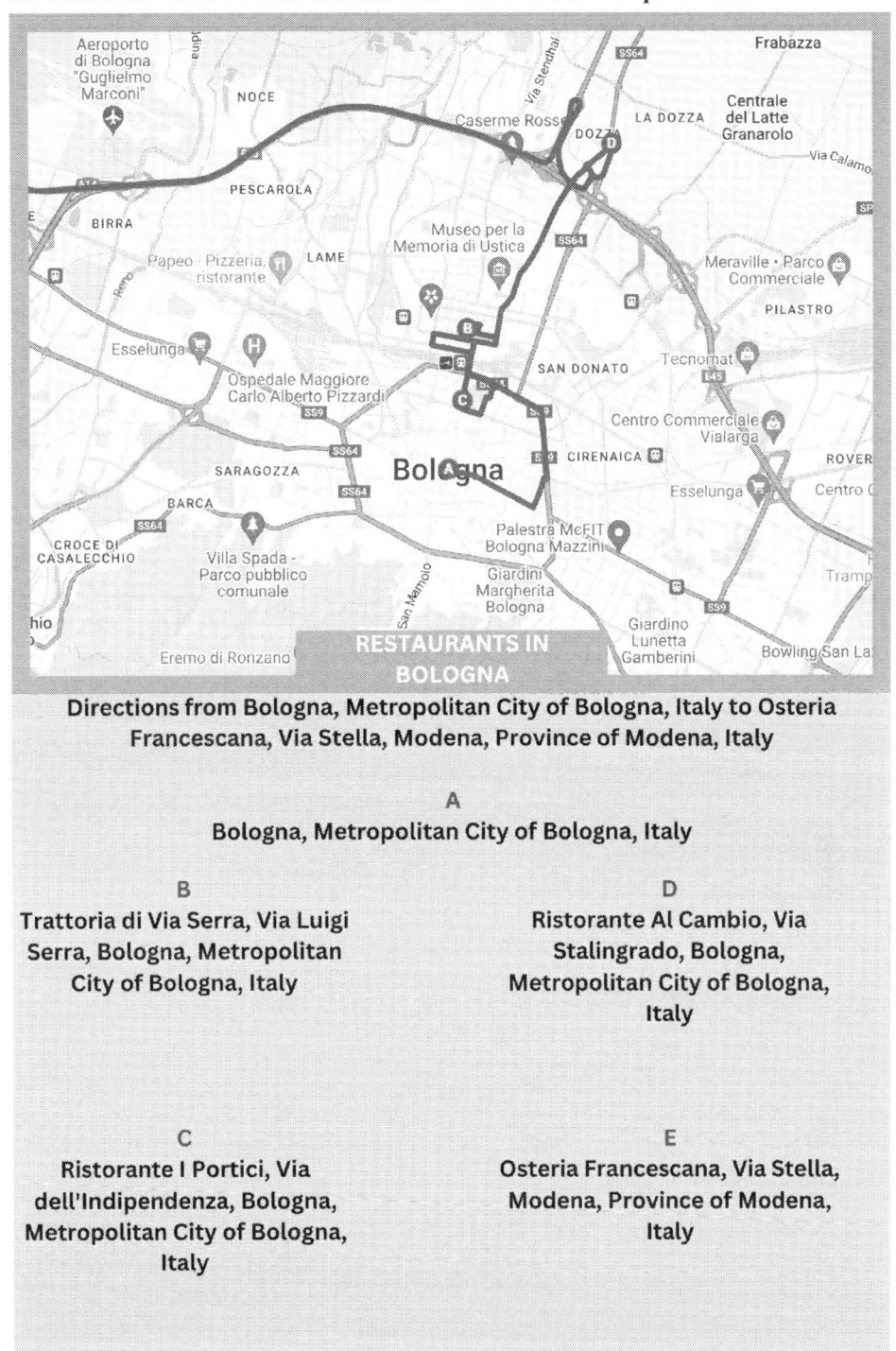

Directions from Bologna, Metropolitan City of Bologna, Italy to Osteria Francescana, Via Stella, Modena, Province of Modena, Italy

A
Bologna, Metropolitan City of Bologna, Italy

B
Trattoria di Via Serra, Via Luigi Serra, Bologna, Metropolitan City of Bologna, Italy

D
Ristorante Al Cambio, Via Stalingrado, Bologna, Metropolitan City of Bologna, Italy

C
Ristorante I Portici, Via dell'Indipendenza, Bologna, Metropolitan City of Bologna, Italy

E
Osteria Francescana, Via Stella, Modena, Province of Modena, Italy

Amidst the labyrinthine streets and ancient architecture, Bologna boasts a constellation of Michelin-starred restaurants that promise an unparalleled gastronomic journey. From innovative culinary creations to time-honored traditions, these establishments elevate dining to an art form, captivating the senses and tantalizing the palate. Let us delve into the realm of Michelin-starred gastronomic experiences in Bologna, where each bite is a symphony of flavors and every meal a celebration of culinary excellence.

Trattoria di Via Serra

Trattoria di Via Serra epitomizes the essence of traditional Italian cuisine with a modern twist. Awarded a Michelin star for its exceptional culinary offerings, this charming trattoria welcomes guests with its warm ambiance and impeccable service. Chef Marco Marocchi's innovative interpretations of classic dishes showcase the finest seasonal ingredients sourced from local producers, ensuring a dining experience that is both flavorful and sustainable. Prices at Trattoria di Via Serra typically range from €50-€80 per person for a multi-course tasting menu, making it an indulgent yet accessible choice for those seeking an authentic taste of Bologna's culinary legacy. Reservations are highly recommended, especially during peak dining hours, to secure a table at this culinary gem.

Ristorante I Portici

Perched beneath the majestic porticoes that line Bologna's historic Via Indipendenza, Ristorante I Portici exudes an air of timeless elegance and sophistication. Boasting a Michelin star for its creative culinary offerings, this acclaimed restaurant enchants guests with its fusion of traditional Italian flavors and contemporary flair. Chef Alessandro Dal Degan's meticulously crafted dishes, inspired by seasonal ingredients and culinary traditions, take diners on a sensory journey through the diverse landscapes of Italy. Prices at Ristorante I Portici typically range from €80-€120 per person for a tasting menu, reflecting the restaurant's commitment to culinary excellence and unparalleled dining experiences. Visitors are advised to dress smartly and make reservations in advance to secure a coveted spot at this gastronomic haven, where every meal is a work of art.

Osteria Francescana

For those with a penchant for culinary adventure and gastronomic innovation, Osteria Francescana beckons as a mecca of haute cuisine in the heart of Modena, just a short distance from Bologna. Helmed by acclaimed chef Massimo Bottura, whose avant-garde creations have earned the restaurant three Michelin stars and the title of "Best Restaurant in the World" by The World's 50 Best Restaurants, Osteria Francescana promises an unforgettable dining experience. Chef Bottura's visionary approach to Italian cuisine transcends tradition, blending art, history, and culture to create culinary masterpieces that defy convention and tantalize the senses. Prices at Osteria Francescana start from €250-€350 per person for a tasting menu, reflecting the restaurant's status as a global culinary destination. Advanced reservations are essential, as tables are in high demand, with waiting lists extending months in advance. Visitors embarking on this culinary pilgrimage are advised to prepare for an immersive gastronomic journey that transcends the boundaries of taste and perception.

Da Gianni

Da Gianni offers a taste of rustic charm and culinary excellence. Awarded a Michelin star for its authentic regional cuisine, this family-owned trattoria captivates diners with its warm hospitality and farm-to-table ethos. Chef Gianni's dedication to showcasing the bounty of Emilia-Romagna's land and sea is evident in every dish, from delicate seafood risottos to hearty meat stews infused with aromatic herbs and spices. Prices at Da Gianni typically range from €40-€60 per person for a multi-course tasting menu, making it an affordable yet indulgent choice for those seeking an authentic taste of the Italian countryside.

Reservations are recommended, especially on weekends, to ensure a memorable dining experience at this hidden gem of culinary excellence.

Al Cambio

Located in the charming town of Bologna, Al Cambio is a culinary oasis that celebrates the rich culinary traditions of Emilia-Romagna with a modern twist. Awarded a Michelin star for its innovative approach to Italian cuisine, this stylish restaurant offers a sensory journey through the flavors of the region, from creamy risottos to succulent grilled meats. Chef Andrea Incerti Vezzani's creative reinterpretations of classic dishes showcase the finest seasonal ingredients sourced from local producers, ensuring a dining experience that is both authentic and inventive. Prices at Al Cambio typically range from €60-€100 per person for a tasting menu, reflecting the restaurant's commitment to culinary excellence and gastronomic innovation. Visitors are advised to make reservations in advance to secure a table at this culinary hotspot, where tradition meets innovation in every dish.

CHAPTER 7
DAY TRIPS AND EXCURSIONS

Directions from Bologna, Metropolitan City of Bologna, Italy to Florence, Metropolitan City of Florence, Italy

A
Bologna, Metropolitan City of Bologna, Italy

B
Modena, Province of Modena, Italy

E
Parma, Province of Parma, Italy

C
Enzo Ferrari Museum, Via Paolo Ferrari, Modena, Province of Modena, Italy

F
Este Castle, Largo Castello, Ferrara, Province of Ferrara, Italy

D
Ravenna, Province of Ravenna, Italy

G
Florence, Metropolitan City of Florence, Italy

7.1 Modena and the Ferrari Museum

Bologna serves as an excellent starting point for an enriching day trip to Modena and the illustrious Ferrari Museum. As you begin your journey from Bologna to Modena, prepare to be captivated by the picturesque scenery of the Italian countryside. The approximately 40-kilometer distance between the two cities promises a delightful drive, offering travelers a glimpse into the charming landscapes of the Emilia-Romagna region.

Savoring the Culinary Delights of Modena

Upon arriving in Modena, travelers are greeted by a city renowned for its culinary excellence. Take the time to indulge in the local gastronomic delights, including the world-famous balsamic vinegar and delectable Parmigiano Reggiano cheese. Wander through the bustling streets adorned with quaint cafes and trattorias, where the aroma of freshly prepared pasta dishes fills the air. Immerse yourself in the rich culinary heritage of Modena, and savor the flavors that have earned the city its esteemed reputation.

Exploring Modena's Architectural Splendors

Modena boasts a wealth of architectural treasures that offer insight into its rich history and cultural significance. Marvel at the majestic Modena Cathedral, a UNESCO World Heritage site renowned for its Romanesque beauty and intricate marble façade. Delve into the city's past as you stroll through the charming Piazza Grande, adorned with elegant palaces and historic buildings that showcase Modena's architectural prowess. Explore the winding streets of the old town, where each corner reveals hidden gems waiting to be discovered.

The Ferrari Museum Experience

No visit to Modena would be complete without a pilgrimage to the Ferrari Museum, a Mecca for automotive enthusiasts and aficionados alike. Situated in the nearby town of Maranello, the museum offers an immersive journey into the iconic world of Ferrari, showcasing a remarkable collection of vintage cars, racing memorabilia, and interactive exhibits. Witness the evolution of automotive engineering as you admire legendary Ferrari models and learn about the brand's storied history. From Formula 1 legends to road-going supercars, the Ferrari Museum promises an unforgettable experience for visitors of all ages.

7.2 Ravenna and its Mosaics

Embarking on a journey from the vibrant city of Bologna, travelers are presented with a myriad of enchanting day trips, each promising an immersive experience in history, culture, and art. Among these, a visit to Ravenna stands out as a captivating excursion, offering a glimpse into the rich tapestry of Byzantine heritage through its exquisite mosaics. Ravenna, located approximately 80 kilometers east of Bologna, is easily accessible by both train and car, making it an ideal destination for a day trip.

Exploring Ravenna's Mosaics

Upon arrival in Ravenna, visitors are greeted by a city steeped in history, with its crowning jewels being the UNESCO-listed mosaics adorning its churches and monuments. The city's mosaic artistry, dating back to the 5th and 6th centuries, serves as a testament to its illustrious past as the capital of the Western Roman Empire and later the Byzantine Empire.

Basilica di San Vitale

One of the foremost attractions in Ravenna is the Basilica di San Vitale, a masterpiece of Byzantine architecture adorned with dazzling mosaics. Stepping into this sacred space, visitors are enveloped in a kaleidoscope of colors and intricate designs, depicting biblical scenes, saints, and emperors. The ethereal beauty of the mosaics, illuminated by soft light filtering through stained glass windows, transports visitors to a bygone era of artistic splendor.

Mausoleum of Galla Placidia

Another gem in Ravenna's mosaic crown is the Mausoleum of Galla Placidia, a small yet exquisitely decorated structure renowned for its celestial mosaics. The interior of the mausoleum is adorned with intricate patterns and symbols, evoking a sense of wonder and reverence. Visitors are captivated by the interplay of light and shadow, which accentuates the delicate craftsmanship of the mosaics, depicting scenes from the Old and New Testaments.

Basilica di Sant'Apollinare Nuovo

Continuing the mosaic trail, travelers are drawn to the Basilica di Sant'Apollinare Nuovo, an architectural marvel adorned with a vast mosaic frieze spanning its nave. The vibrant mosaics narrate scenes from the life of Christ, accompanied by a procession of martyrs and virgins, offering insight into Ravenna's Christian heritage. As visitors gaze upon these ancient artworks, they are transported back in time, marveling at the skill and devotion of the craftsmen who brought them to life.

Cost of Transportation

The cost of transportation from Bologna to Ravenna varies depending on the mode of travel and ticket class chosen. Train tickets typically range from €10 to €20 per person for a one-way journey, while car rental prices may vary based on vehicle type and rental duration. Additionally, visitors should budget for entrance fees to Ravenna's monuments, with individual tickets priced between €5 and €10 per attraction, or opt for a combined ticket for comprehensive access to multiple sites.

7.3 Parma and its Culinary Heritage

Bologna serves as an excellent gateway to explore the gastronomic delights of its neighboring cities. Among these gems, Parma stands out with its rich culinary heritage, offering a tantalizing array of flavors and experiences awaiting curious travelers. Embark on a journey from Bologna to Parma, immersing yourself in a culinary adventure that promises to delight the senses and leave a lasting impression.

Embracing Proximity

Traveling from Bologna to Parma is not only a journey of gastronomic discovery but also a seamless excursion facilitated by the efficient transportation network of the region. With a distance of approximately 90 kilometers separating the two cities, travelers have multiple transportation options at their disposal. The most convenient and time-efficient method is undoubtedly by train, with frequent services connecting Bologna Centrale Station to Parma Station in under an hour. The cost of a one-way train ticket typically ranges from €10 to €20, depending on the class and time of booking, offering excellent value for money.

A Gourmet Pilgrimage

Upon arrival in Parma, visitors are greeted by an enchanting cityscape adorned with architectural marvels, picturesque streets, and a palpable sense of culinary tradition. As the birthplace of Parmigiano Reggiano cheese, Parma Ham (Prosciutto di Parma), and balsamic vinegar, the city beckons gastronomes to indulge in a gastronomic pilgrimage unlike any other.

The King of Cheeses

No visit to Parma is complete without a visit to a local cheese factory, where the art of crafting Parmigiano Reggiano comes to life. Witness the meticulous process of cheese-making, from the curdling of milk to the aging of wheels, and savor the distinct flavors of this esteemed cheese during a guided tasting session. Visitors can purchase freshly cut wedges to take home as a delectable souvenir of their culinary journey.

Prosciutto di Parma

For aficionados of cured meats, a visit to a traditional prosciutto factory is a must-do experience in Parma. Delve into the centuries-old techniques of salting, curing, and aging that transform pork legs into the iconic Prosciutto di Parma. Indulge in a tasting session that showcases the delicate balance of sweet and savory flavors, paired perfectly with local wines and artisanal bread.

Balsamic Vinegar

Discover the secret behind the exquisite taste of authentic balsamic vinegar during a guided tour of a traditional acetaia (vinegar cellar). Learn about the lengthy aging process that imbues balsamic vinegar with its complex flavors and aromatic bouquet, culminating in a tasting session that reveals the depth and sophistication of this culinary treasure. Visitors can also explore the versatility of balsamic vinegar in cooking during hands-on workshops led by local experts.

Dining in Parma

After a day of culinary exploration, savor the flavors of Parma's gastronomic heritage at one of the city's renowned trattorias or osterias. Feast on regional specialties such as tortelli d'erbetta (herb-filled pasta), cappelletti in brodo (stuffed pasta in broth), and tagliatelle al ragù (pasta with meat sauce), accompanied by fine wines sourced from nearby vineyards. End your culinary odyssey on a sweet note with a taste of torta fritta (fried dough) served with acacia honey or fruit preserves.

7.4 Ferrara and the Este Castle

Set amidst the enchanting landscapes of the Emilia-Romagna region, Ferrara beckons travelers to embark on a captivating day trip from Bologna. As you embark on this cultural odyssey, prepare to be mesmerized by the timeless charm of Ferrara, a city steeped in history and adorned with architectural splendor. The approximately 50-kilometer journey from Bologna to Ferrara offers travelers a scenic route through the picturesque countryside, providing a glimpse into the rustic beauty of rural Italy.

Immersing Yourself in Ferrara's Rich Heritage

Upon arriving in Ferrara, travelers are greeted by a city steeped in history and brimming with cultural heritage. Take the time to explore the historic city center, a UNESCO World Heritage site renowned for its well-preserved medieval architecture and Renaissance masterpieces. Wander through the cobblestone streets lined with elegant palaces, charming piazzas, and quaint cafes, immersing yourself in the timeless ambiance of Ferrara. Discover the legacy of the Este family, who ruled over the city for centuries and left behind a legacy of artistic and architectural excellence.

Exploring the Magnificent Este Castle

No visit to Ferrara would be complete without exploring the iconic Este Castle, a symbol of the city's illustrious past and grandeur. Situated at the heart of Ferrara's historic center, the Este Castle stands as a testament to the power and prestige of the Este dynasty. Step back in time as you wander through the castle's imposing walls and majestic courtyards, marveling at its formidable ramparts and intricate architectural details. Explore the castle's interior, where ornate frescoes, lavish furnishings, and ancient artifacts offer insight into Ferrara's rich cultural heritage. From the medieval dungeons to the opulent ducal chambers, the Este Castle promises a journey through time that is both educational and awe-inspiring.

7.5 Florence: The Cradle of the Renaissance

Amidst the rolling hills of Tuscany lies Florence, the quintessential cradle of the Renaissance. From Bologna, travelers are presented with an enticing array of day trip opportunities to this cultural mecca, where every cobblestone street whispers tales of artistic genius and historical grandeur. Embarking on this journey promises an immersive experience in the heart of Italy's cultural heritage, where the legacy of luminaries such as Michelangelo, Leonardo da Vinci, and Botticelli comes to life amidst the city's iconic landmarks and world-class museums.

Transportation and Distance

The journey from Bologna to Florence is both convenient and efficient, with frequent train services connecting the two cities in under an hour. Departing from Bologna Centrale station, travelers can enjoy a scenic ride through the picturesque Tuscan countryside, arriving at Florence's Santa Maria Novella station, conveniently located within walking distance of the city center. For those preferring the flexibility of a self-driven excursion, the approximately 100-kilometer journey can be completed in just over an hour by car, offering the added advantage of exploring the scenic beauty of the Tuscan landscape along the way.

Immersing in Florence's Renaissance Treasures

Upon arrival in Florence, visitors are greeted by a city steeped in artistic grandeur, where every street corner unveils a masterpiece waiting to be discovered. The historic center of Florence, a UNESCO World Heritage Site, serves as the perfect starting point for exploration, with its labyrinthine streets leading to iconic landmarks such as the Florence Cathedral, Ponte Vecchio, and Piazza della Signoria.

Uffizi Gallery

A highlight of any visit to Florence is a pilgrimage to the Uffizi Gallery, home to one of the most extensive collections of Renaissance art in the world. Here, visitors can marvel at masterpieces by the likes of Botticelli, Michelangelo, and Raphael, as they trace the evolution of art from the medieval period to the height of the Renaissance. From the ethereal beauty of Botticelli's "The Birth of Venus" to the monumental grandeur of Michelangelo's "Tondo Doni," the Uffizi Gallery offers an unparalleled journey through the annals of art history.

Florence Cathedral (Duomo)

Dominating the city's skyline with its majestic dome, the Florence Cathedral, or Duomo, is an architectural marvel that epitomizes the Renaissance spirit. Ascending the 463 steps to the top of Brunelleschi's dome rewards visitors with panoramic views of Florence and the surrounding Tuscan landscape, while the interior of the cathedral dazzles with its intricate frescoes and marble adornments.

Accademia Gallery

No visit to Florence would be complete without paying homage to Michelangelo's iconic masterpiece, "David," housed within the hallowed halls of the Accademia Gallery. As visitors stand in awe before this towering marble sculpture, they are transported back in time to the pinnacle of Renaissance artistry, marveling at the sculptor's unparalleled skill and mastery of form.

Cost of Transportation

The cost of transportation from Bologna to Florence varies depending on the mode of travel and ticket class chosen. Train tickets typically range from €15 to €30 per person for a one-way journey, with discounts available for advance bookings and youth travelers.

CHAPTER 8
ENTERTAINMENT AND NIGHTLIFE

8.1 Piazza Maggiore: Cafés and Aperitivo Spots

Piazza Maggiore, a bustling square that transforms into a hub of entertainment and nightlife as dusk descends. Here, among its cobblestone streets and ancient buildings, visitors can embark on an enchanting journey through various entertainment venues, each offering a unique glimpse into the city's vibrant soul.

Cafés

As twilight settles over Piazza Maggiore, the aroma of freshly brewed coffee wafts through the air, inviting passersby to indulge in Bologna's rich café culture. Among the cobblestone lanes, quaint cafés beckon with their warm ambiance and exquisite blends. One such gem is Caffè Zanarini, a historic establishment renowned for its decadent pastries and aromatic espresso. Here, amidst elegant décor and the gentle hum of conversation, patrons can immerse themselves in the timeless charm of Italian café culture.

Aperitivo Spots

For those seeking a leisurely evening reprieve, Piazza Maggiore offers an array of enticing aperitivo spots where locals and visitors alike gather to unwind and socialize. Nestled in the heart of the square is Osteria del Sole, a beloved haunt cherished for its rustic ambiance and extensive selection of wines. Here, amidst weathered wooden tables and flickering candlelight, guests can indulge in a delightful array of local cheeses, cured meats, and artisanal snacks, perfectly complemented by the velvety notes of regional wines.

Live Music Venues

As night falls over Piazza Maggiore, the city's musical heartbeat quickens, luring enthusiasts to its intimate live music venues nestled within its historic alleys. At Jazz Club Torrione, the sultry strains of jazz melodies fill the air, drawing aficionados to its cozy confines. Here, beneath the glow of dimmed lights, guests can lose themselves in the rhythmic pulse of live performances, savoring each soulful note as it dances through the night.

Cocktail Bars

For those in search of libations and nocturnal delights, Piazza Maggiore boasts an eclectic array of cocktail bars where mixology meets artistry. Tucked away in a secluded corner is Sottotetto Rooftop Lounge, an urban oasis offering panoramic views of the city skyline. Here, amidst chic décor and ambient beats, mixologists craft signature cocktails infused with local flavors, inviting guests to raise a glass to the evening's revelry as they bask in the city's nocturnal allure.

Theater and Cinema

As the night unfolds, Piazza Maggiore becomes a stage for cultural exploration, with theaters and cinemas showcasing a diverse tapestry of performances and screenings. At Cinema Lumière, cinephiles can immerse themselves in a world of cinematic wonders, with curated film festivals and screenings that celebrate the art of storytelling. Meanwhile, Teatro Comunale di Bologna invites audiences to embark on a theatrical journey through captivating performances ranging from classical opera to avant-garde theater, captivating hearts and minds with each mesmerizing act.

8.2 Live Music Venues and Jazz Clubs

As the sun dips below the horizon, the city transforms into a haven for music aficionados and nocturnal wanderers alike, beckoning with its array of live music venues and jazz clubs. Embark on a nocturnal odyssey through Bologna's streets, where the melodies are as rich as the city's culinary offerings.

Cantina Bentivoglio

Tucked away in the medieval heart of Bologna lies Cantina Bentivoglio, a legendary jazz club that has been serenading patrons for over four decades. Stepping into its dimly lit ambiance feels like entering a portal to another era, where the air is thick with the sultry notes of live jazz performances. From established artists to up-and-coming talents, the stage of Cantina Bentivoglio hosts a diverse array of musicians, ensuring an unforgettable evening of rhythm and soul. While prices vary depending on the event, the experience is priceless, transporting visitors to the heyday of jazz in an intimate setting.

Bravo Caffè

For a sensory journey that tantalizes both the palate and the ears, Bravo Caffè is the quintessential destination. This eclectic venue seamlessly blends gastronomy with live music, offering a symphony of flavors and melodies. Whether you're craving the smooth harmonies of jazz or the upbeat rhythms of blues, Bravo Caffè delivers an unparalleled experience. While prices may lean towards the higher end, the fusion of exquisite cuisine and top-notch entertainment ensures that every euro spent is a testament to indulgence.

Locomotiv Club

In the vibrant district of Bolognina, Locomotiv Club reigns supreme as a bastion of underground music and avant-garde performances. This gritty yet inviting venue pulsates with energy, drawing in a diverse crowd of music enthusiasts and trendsetters. From indie rock bands to electronic DJs, Locomotiv Club showcases an eclectic lineup that pushes the boundaries of conventional nightlife. With affordable ticket prices and a laid-back atmosphere, this is the go-to spot for those seeking an authentic glimpse into Bologna's thriving alternative scene.

Covo Club

Covo Club stands as a testament to the city's vibrant cultural tapestry. This intimate venue exudes a sense of camaraderie, welcoming both seasoned regulars and curious newcomers with open arms. With its diverse lineup of live music, spanning genres from rock to reggae, Covo Club embodies the spirit of inclusivity and artistic expression. Affordable entry fees and a warm, convivial atmosphere make it the perfect setting for forging new connections and creating lasting memories.

Freakout Club

For those with a penchant for the unconventional, Freakout Club offers a kaleidoscopic journey through Bologna's underground music scene. Situated in the dynamic neighborhood of San Vitale, this avant-garde venue showcases a diverse array of musical genres, from experimental noise to psychedelic rock. With its eclectic lineup of local and international artists, Freakout Club promises an immersive sonic experience unlike any other. While ticket prices may vary depending on the event, the opportunity to explore the fringes of musical expression is priceless.

8.3 Teatro Comunale di Bologna: Opera and Theater Performances

Teatro Comunale di Bologna stands as a beacon of artistic excellence and historical significance. This iconic venue invites you to immerse yourself in its world, offering an experience that transcends the ordinary. Let's embark on a journey through its various locations and uncover the magic that awaits within its walls.

The Grandeur of the Main Auditorium

As you step into the Main Auditorium of the Teatro Comunale di Bologna, you're immediately enveloped by a sense of grandeur and timeless elegance. The opulent décor, with its gilded balconies and plush red velvet seats, transports you to a bygone era of operatic splendor. Here, the world's finest voices and musicians come together to create unforgettable performances. The acoustics, meticulously designed to perfection, ensure that every note resonates with clarity and power. Whether you're attending a classic opera or a contemporary concert, the Main Auditorium promises an experience that is both visually and sonically spectacular. Ticket prices vary depending on the performance and seating choice, with options ranging from affordable balconies to premium front-row seats, ensuring that every visitor can find a suitable option.

Intimate Performances at the Sala Bibiena

For those seeking a more intimate and personal encounter with the arts, the Sala Bibiena offers a perfect retreat. This smaller, yet equally enchanting, space is ideal for chamber music concerts, solo recitals, and experimental theater. The Sala Bibiena's unique charm lies in its ability to create a close connection between the performers and the audience, making each event feel like a private gathering. The elegant design and warm, inviting ambiance add to the overall sense of intimacy. Ticket prices are generally more accessible, making it a wonderful option for those looking to explore new forms of artistic expression without compromising on quality.

The Historical Archive

A visit to the Teatro Comunale di Bologna would be incomplete without exploring its Historical Archive. This treasure trove of documents, costumes, set designs, and photographs offers a fascinating glimpse into the theater's storied past. As you delve into the archive, you'll uncover stories of legendary performances, celebrated artists, and the evolution of theatrical production over the centuries. The archive is a testament to the theater's enduring legacy and its pivotal role in the cultural life of Bologna. Access to the archive is often included with special guided tours, which are reasonably priced and provide a deeper understanding of the theater's historical significance.

The Enchanting Foyer: The Foyer of the Teatro Comunale di Bologna is more than just a waiting area; it's a work of art in itself. With its stunning frescoes, elegant chandeliers, and tasteful décor, the Foyer sets the tone for the evening ahead. It's a place where patrons can gather before a performance, savor a glass of prosecco, and soak in the atmosphere of anticipation. The Foyer often hosts pre-show talks, exhibitions, and social events, adding an extra layer of engagement to your visit. Entry to the Foyer is typically included with your ticket, making it a delightful bonus to your evening at the theater.

The Open-Air Arena: For a truly unique experience, the Open-Air Arena adjacent to the Teatro Comunale di Bologna offers performances under the stars. This modern addition to the theater complex provides a stunning contrast to the historical interiors, blending contemporary design with the natural beauty of the surroundings. During the warmer months, the Open-Air Arena hosts a variety of performances, from opera and ballet to jazz concerts and theatrical productions. The setting is perfect for enjoying a summer evening, with the stars overhead and the enchanting sounds of live performance filling the air. Ticket prices for the Open-Air Arena are generally competitive, with many options available for those looking to enjoy a memorable evening without breaking the bank.

8.4 Bars and Wine Bars

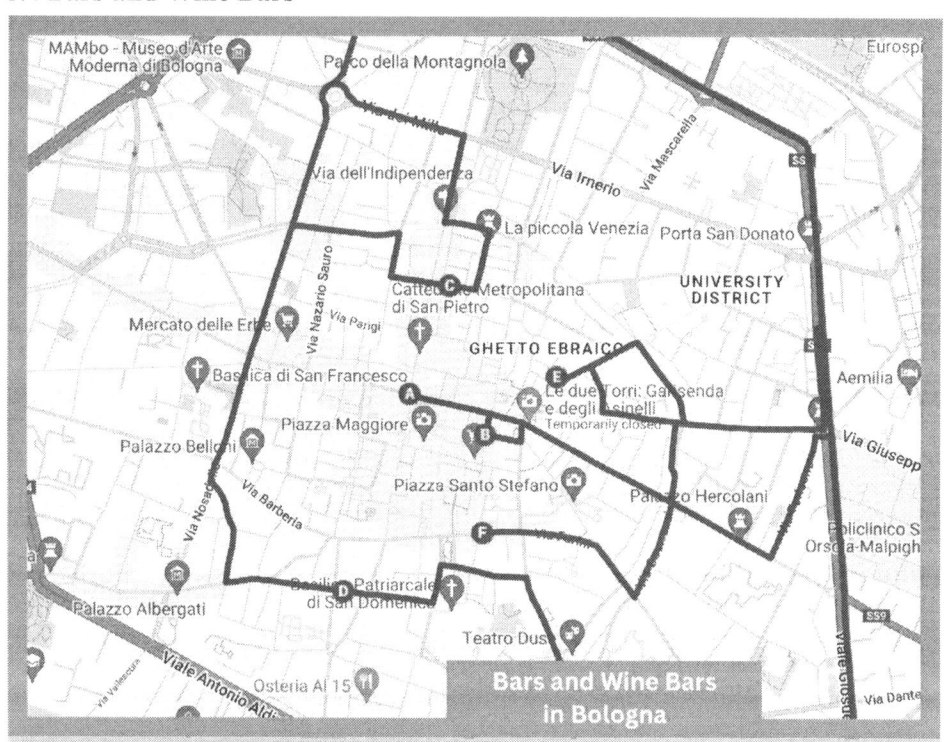

Directions from Bologna, Metropolitan City of Bologna, Italy to Casa Minghetti, Piazza Minghetti, Bologna, Metropolitan City of Bologna, Italy

A
Bologna, Metropolitan City of Bologna, Italy

B
Osteria del Sole, Vicolo Ranocchi, Bologna, Metropolitan City of Bologna, Italy

C
Enoteca Italiana, Via Marsala, Bologna, Metropolitan City of Bologna, Italy

D
È cucina marrett, Via Urbana, Bologna, Metropolitan City of Bologna, Italy

E
Lab 16, Via Zamboni, Bologna, Metropolitan City of Bologna, Italy

F
Casa Minghetti, Piazza Minghetti, Bologna, Metropolitan City of Bologna, Italy

Amidst its labyrinthine streets and centuries-old architecture, lies a treasure trove of bars and wine bars waiting to be discovered. Each establishment boasts its own unique charm, offering visitors a tantalizing glimpse into the city's vibrant social scene and rich culinary heritage. From cozy taverns steeped in history to chic wine bars exuding contemporary flair, Bologna promises an unforgettable journey through its spirited nightlife.

Osteria del Sole

Osteria del Sole stands as a testament to the city's timeless allure. Stepping through its weathered doorway, visitors are transported back in time to a bygone era, where wooden beams and antique furnishings create an ambiance of rustic elegance. Here, amidst the gentle clink of glasses and the murmur of conversation, patrons can savor an array of local wines and traditional aperitifs, forging connections and sharing stories late into the night.

Enoteca Italiana

For those with a penchant for the finer things in life, Enoteca Italiana beckons with its exquisite selection of wines and unparalleled elegance. Tucked away within a historic palazzo, this upscale wine bar invites guests to embark on a sensory journey through Italy's renowned wine regions, with knowledgeable sommeliers guiding them through each tasting experience. From velvety Barolos to crisp Pinot Grigios, every sip reveals a new dimension of flavor, tantalizing the palate and igniting the imagination.

Tamburini Vino e Cucina

Amidst the bustling streets of Bologna's Quadrilatero district lies Tamburini Vino e Cucina, a culinary institution beloved by locals and visitors alike. Here, amidst shelves laden with artisanal delicacies and gleaming bottles of wine, guests can indulge in the timeless flavors of Emilia-Romagna. From platters of creamy Parmigiano Reggiano to plates of savory prosciutto, each dish is a testament to the region's rich gastronomic heritage, while the expertly curated wine selection offers the perfect accompaniment to every bite.

Bohemian Chic at Lab 16

Tucked away in a quaint courtyard off the beaten path, Lab 16 exudes an air of bohemian charm, drawing inquisitive souls with its eclectic décor and laid-back ambiance. Here, amidst mismatched furniture and whimsical artwork, patrons can unwind with a glass of artisanal beer or sip on creative cocktails infused with local ingredients. Whether lounging on plush sofas or mingling with fellow travelers, Lab 16 promises an immersive experience that captures the essence of Bologna's vibrant social scene.

Casa Minghetti

Perched atop a historic palazzo overlooking the city skyline, Casa Minghetti offers a sophisticated retreat for discerning connoisseurs. As the sun sets over Bologna, guests ascend to the rooftop terrace, where panoramic views and plush seating await. Against this breathtaking backdrop, mixologists craft inventive cocktails inspired by the flavors of the season, while sommeliers curate wine pairings that elevate each sip to new heights. With its blend of modern luxury and old-world charm, Casa Minghetti invites guests to savor the moment and revel in the magic of Bologna's vibrant nightlife scene.

8.5 Festivals and Events

Bologna, with its rich history and dynamic spirit, beckons travelers to immerse themselves in its vibrant calendar of festivities. From traditional celebrations steeped in centuries-old traditions to avant-garde events that push the boundaries of creativity, there's something for everyone to discover in this captivating city.

Bologna Jazz Festival

Each November, the city comes alive with the soul-stirring melodies of the Bologna Jazz Festival. Held in various venues across the city, this internationally acclaimed event attracts jazz aficionados from near and far. From intimate club performances to grand concerts in historic theaters, the festival showcases a diverse lineup of artists, spanning genres from traditional jazz to avant-garde fusion. Beyond the music, attendees can partake in workshops, film screenings, and culinary experiences, making it a multifaceted celebration of both sound and culture.

MortadellaBò

For food lovers, MortadellaBò is a culinary pilgrimage not to be missed. Held annually in September, this festival pays homage to Bologna's most iconic delicacy: mortadella. Visitors flock to Piazza Maggiore, where local producers showcase their finest creations, offering tantalizing tastings and demonstrations. From traditional mortadella sandwiches to innovative culinary creations, the festival is a feast for the senses. Live music, street performers, and artisanal markets add to the festive atmosphere, making MortadellaBò a true celebration of Bologna's gastronomic heritage.

Arte Fiera

In late January, Bologna becomes a hub of artistic innovation with the arrival of Arte Fiera. As one of Italy's oldest and most prestigious art fairs, Arte Fiera attracts collectors, curators, and art enthusiasts from around the globe. Held at the BolognaFiere exhibition center, the fair features a curated selection of contemporary artworks, ranging from paintings and sculptures to multimedia installations. In addition to the main exhibition, visitors can explore special projects, panel discussions, and guided tours, offering a comprehensive insight into the ever-evolving world of contemporary art.

Cinema Ritrovato

Film buffs rejoice at the arrival of Cinema Ritrovato, a cinematic extravaganza that takes place every June in Bologna's historic theaters and outdoor venues. Dedicated to the preservation and celebration of classic cinema, this internationally renowned festival showcases a curated selection of rare and restored films from around the world. From silent masterpieces to golden-age classics, Cinema Ritrovato offers a unique opportunity to experience cinema history on the big screen. Q&A sessions with filmmakers, archival presentations, and live musical accompaniments enrich the viewing experience, making it a must-attend event for cinephiles of all ages.

Bologna Children's Book Fair

For families and book lovers alike, the Bologna Children's Book Fair is a magical journey into the world of storytelling and imagination. Held annually in April, this internationally acclaimed event brings together publishers, authors, illustrators, and literary enthusiasts to celebrate children's literature in all its forms. From captivating book signings to interactive workshops and storytelling sessions, the fair offers endless opportunities for young readers to discover new worlds and ignite their passion for reading. With its vibrant atmosphere and diverse programming, the Bologna Children's Book Fair is a testament to the enduring power of storytelling to inspire, educate, and unite.

CONCLUSION AND RECOMMENDATIONS

As we draw the curtains on our exploration of Bologna, it's evident that this city is more than just a destination; it's an experience that lingers in the soul long after the journey ends. From the majestic towers that punctuate the skyline to the labyrinthine streets steeped in history, Bologna is a treasure trove waiting to be discovered. As you navigate its cobblestone alleys and vibrant piazzas, you'll find yourself enchanted by the city's timeless charm and dynamic spirit.

Recommendations for the Discerning Traveler:

Embrace the Aperitivo Culture: Bologna's aperitivo scene is legendary, offering a delightful array of pre-dinner drinks and snacks. Look out for local favorites like spritz and negroni, accompanied by a tantalizing selection of antipasti. Head to the university district for the best deals and lively atmosphere.

Get Lost in the Quadrilatero: The Quadrilatero, Bologna's medieval market district, is a maze of narrow streets brimming with artisanal shops, bustling markets, and hidden gems. Take your time to wander off the beaten path and discover charming cafes, traditional trattorias, and family-owned boutiques.

Rise Above the City: For panoramic views of Bologna's terracotta rooftops and historic landmarks, climb to the top of the Asinelli Tower. Be prepared for a steep ascent, but the breathtaking vistas from the top make it well worth the effort. For a quieter alternative, head to the nearby San Michele in Bosco for equally stunning views.

Sample Bologna's Culinary Delights: Don't leave Bologna without indulging in its culinary delights. From creamy tagliatelle al ragù to savory tortellini en brodo, the city's food scene is a gastronomic paradise. Venture beyond the tourist hotspots to discover authentic trattorias and family-run osterias serving up traditional recipes passed down through generations.

Immerse Yourself in the Local Culture: Bologna's cultural heritage is as diverse as it is rich, with museums, galleries, and historical sites waiting to be explored. Take a guided tour of the Basilica of San Petronio to uncover its fascinating history, or wander through the city's street art scene for a contemporary perspective on Bologna's artistic identity.

Bologna has revealed itself as a destination that transcends mere sightseeing. So, as you carry the essence of Bologna with you on your onward journey, remember that its doors are always open, ready to welcome you back with open arms. Until we meet again, arrivederci, and may the spirit of Bologna accompany you wherever your travels may lead!

Printed in Great Britain
by Amazon